Joy and Strength

365 Devotions
for Grief and Loss

BroadStreet
PUBLISHING

BroadStreet Publishing Group, LLC.
Savage, Minnesota, USA
Broadstreetpublishing.com

Joy and Strength

978-1-4245-6228-2
978-1-4245-6229-9 (eBook)

Devotions composed by Sara Perry.

Design by Chris Garborg | garborgdesign.com
Edited by Michelle Winger | literallyprecise.com

Printed in China.

21 22 23 24 25 7 6 5 4 3 2 1

For he has not despised
my cries of deep despair.
He didn't look the other way
when I was in pain.
He was there all the time.

PSALM 22:24 TPT

Introduction

God is the best source of comfort you will find. He knows you better than anyone else does, and he is full of understanding for every situation. Some days your heart may be filled with grief, some may hold a flicker of hope, and on others you might ache with desperate need. Lay your heart at the Father's feet and wait for his compassionate response. You can trust him completely.

It is important in your process of grief to recognize your depth of loss and express it in whatever way you can in the moment. Let God be your strength as you cry out to him. He is listening to every word you say, and he longs to reach out and draw you in close.

January

You will call on me
and come and pray to me,
and I will listen to you.

JEREMIAH 29:12 NIV

Eternal Comfort

May our Lord Jesus Christ himself and God our Father, who loved us and by his grace gave us eternal comfort and a wonderful hope, comfort you and strengthen you.

2 THESSALONIANS 2:16-17 NLT

In the tension of hopeful prospects for new beginnings and the pain of loss and disappointment, there is an invitation to take hold of God's steady hand of grace. He offers us relief for our distress. He offers peace of mind for the racing thoughts that cycle back to the taunting what-ifs left in the wake of loss.

Jesus Christ himself is our peace. He is acquainted with suffering. Let us turn our hearts over to his comfort and strength as the Spirit wraps around us with love's soothing embrace. His compassion completely covers us. We can find rest in his comfort today.

Father, I want to know your comforting embrace as I lift my heart toward you. I rely on your strength because I am running out of my own. Surround me with your perfect peace.

Beyond the Pain

*This light momentary affliction is preparing for us an eternal weight
of glory beyond all comparison, as we look not to the things that are
seen but to the things that are unseen. For the things that are seen are
transient, but the things that are unseen are eternal.*

2 Corinthians 4:17-18 esv

When suffering clouds our minds and darkens our days, it can be difficult to imagine a different reality. Though we may feel beaten down by the death of disappointed dreams and hopes that will never materialize the way we had expected, this is not the end of our story.

In a shifting world, where the only certainty we can depend upon is change, let us remember that there is a greater eternal reality awaiting us. God's expansive love carries us through the dark nights into the bright dawn of his mercy. May our eyes look past these temporary troubles to the eternal hope of his glorious kingdom where his light will never dim and our hopes will never be frustrated.

God, I trust that even when I cannot see your goodness and I struggle to believe for lighter days, you are faithful and true. I depend on you for vision. Let me see from your perspective. I need your help.

Called His Own

The LORD will not abandon His people on account of His great name, because the LORD has been pleased to make you a people for Himself.
1 SAMUEL 12:22 NASB

God's great love is not dependent on our reception of it. His compassion does not waver when our hearts grow cold. He is gentle in loving leadership, knowing what we need in every moment. Our questions, our pain, even our accusations do nothing to dissuade his mercy.

He has called us his children. He claims us as his own. It is his parental prerogative to love us at our best and at our worst. We don't need to worry on our hard days that we somehow run the risk of being disowned by our heavenly Father. He will never change his mind, and he will never leave us.

Perfect Father, I am so grateful for the revelation that you will never leave me. I don't want to fight against you today; I want to be held by love. Draw close, God, and let me feel the relief of your presence.

Empowered to Hope

May the God of hope fill you with all joy and peace in believing,
so that you may abound in hope by the power of the Holy Spirit.
ROMANS 15:13 NRSV

When you struggle to grab hold of hope, there is no need to despair. When you run out of your reserves of courage, do not lose heart. You have access to the source of life itself. Where death has rocked your world, the Spirit's life will breathe hope into your heart.

You were never meant to strive to believe. Surrender to the wisdom of God's eternal Word, and the Holy Spirit will empower you with supernatural strength. Joy will be yours again. Peace will be your covering. Does it sound too good to be true? That is the good news that God offers! He will restore you; you will not be left untouched by his resurrection power.

God, I have no hope outside of you. When I struggle to see any goodness, would you empower me to see where you are already at work with your restoration power? I rely on you.

Look to Him

LORD, I know that people's lives are not their own;
it is not for them to direct their steps.
JEREMIAH 10:23 NIV

We cannot escape the sting of suffering in this life. Anyone denying its effects would be deemed a liar. Heartbreak is an unwelcome guest, though it can be used in the refiner's fire to purify us. When grief comes barging through the door of our hearts, will we let it recklessly wreak havoc? Or will we allow our good Father to use it to filter out the impurities of our lives?

There is always an invitation in the pain. With God, death is not simply an ending point. It is an opportunity for rebirth, for resurrection, for new life. Will we let courage lead us into surrender as God does what he alone can do? He is the master restorer.

Lord, I surrender my heart to you today. I invite you into the intense pain of my grief. Comfort me as you purify me in your love. I know that sorrow does not last forever. I trust you.

Held by Love

The LORD is close to the brokenhearted;
he rescues those whose spirits are crushed.
PSALM 34:18 NLT

When you buckle under the weight of your sadness, God, your comforter, is there to lift you up. He is supporting you as your legs give way under the heavy load of grief that you bear. If you remember only one thing today, let it be this: the Lord is near.

He will not let you waste away in your distress. He is your *present* help. He is your shield, your strength, and your defender. He is your rescuer. Even if you cannot sense him, know that he is with you. You cannot escape the grip of his mercy. You are held by love.

Lord, I need to know your nearness. I am desperate for your help, for relief. Spirit, cover me with your peace today. I cannot go on without you. Hold me close in comfort so I can hear the heartbeat of your love over me. I trust that you are here with me.

Help at Hand

Every time they cried out to you in their despair,
you were faithful to deliver them;
you didn't disappoint them.

PSALM 22:5 TPT

In life, we cannot escape the circumstances that inevitably make us feel like we are in over our heads. We cannot fill ourselves with enough courage and wisdom to dismantle what we cannot understand. God is our help whenever we need it. He does not ridicule our weakness, nor does he expect perfection from our efforts.

God is full of strength and mercy; he is a faithful deliverer. He is closer than the breath in your lungs. He is your very source; he is your Creator. Will you stop your striving and let him help you? You don't face any obstacle alone. Cry out to him at any time; your weakness will call on his strength, and he will not disappoint you.

Faithful Father, I call out to you today. I recognize that I have been discouraged by my inability to meet the needs around me. My capacity is more limited than I want to admit. Help me, God. I need you to come through!

Solid Ground

He lifted me out of the pit of despair,
out of the mud and the mire.
He set my feet on solid ground
and steadied me as I walked along.
PSALM 40:2 NLT

There is no shame in recognizing that you cannot lift yourself out of the trenches of despair on your own. God will not leave you to claw at the flimsy ropes of fleeting hope. In your desperation for relief, call out to the one who calls you by name. He is closer than you realize.

Here he is with mercy's anchor. He already has his hand under you, ready to lift you up and out of the mire of despondency. You will find your feet on the firm rock of his unchanging nature. Where you have felt stuck, he will carry you out; your feet will find their footing on the bedrock of his strong love once again as you lean on his steady leadership.

My God, be my strong and constant support. I cannot climb my way out of the grief that tears at my soul, but I know I don't need to. Carry me through until I can stand once more, leaning on your steady countenance.

Shield around Me

You, O Lord, are a shield about me,
my glory, and the lifter of my head.
PSALM 3:3 ESV

When the storms of life rage, God will not leave you to be torn apart by the winds of adversity. He is a shield, a shelter, and a safe place to all who call on his name. He hems you into the garment of his love, hiding you in the commanding compassion of his heart.

The Lord your God surrounds you with the deliverance you have been crying out to receive. He lifts your head every time it drops. Even now, he puts his finger under your chin and beckons you to lift your eyes to his. Can you meet the intensity of his loving gaze? He sees you. He knows what is on your heart even if your lips can't speak it. He is here with kindness and strength.

Loving God, help me see you as you are today. As my heart struggles to comprehend the capacity for pain and joy to coexist, will you give me a glimpse of your pure compassion once again?

Light of Love

He has delivered us from the power of darkness
and conveyed us into the kingdom of the Son of His love.
COLOSSIANS 1:13 NKJV

No matter how dark the day is, there is always a brighter one ahead. Our faithful Father has given us such a strong hope to cling to in the inheritance of his Son. We belong to an everlasting kingdom that is ruled with the law of love as its standard. Let our hearts take hold of the glorious anticipation of the fullness of the freedom that is ours in Christ.

As children of God, we are not bound by fear. We are not shackled by sin and death. We are free in the love of our unrelenting, merciful King. May we not lose hope, for his kingdom will never be shaken. May we live as children of the light, knowing our sorrows are temporary but his power breaks every stronghold. His compassionate kindness knows no end.

Merciful One, I trust that you know exactly where I am. You won't let me be overtaken by the grief I bear. Be with me in the sorrow and deliver me from the overwhelming weightiness that I cannot carry on my own. I need you.

Confident Hope

Faith is confidence in what we hope for
and assurance about what we do not see.
HEBREWS 11:1 NIV

As you turn your awareness toward God today, put away the disappointments of yesterday, even if just for the next few moments. Let the screen of your mind serve as a place of remembrance right now: of God's unstoppable goodness, his breathtaking faithfulness, and attention to detail. Can you recall the confidence you once felt in his kindness toward you?

Though loss may strip you of your comfort, it can never remove the steadfast purposes of your good Father. Even as he mourns with you, holding you close and sharing your pain, he never loses sight of his unwavering intentions. Will you dare look to him now, without the lens of disenchantment clouding your understanding? You will find his attention on you. He is holding you close; let him love you to life in mercy's embrace.

Unchanging One, I look to you today for a fresh perspective of grace. I want to know the grip of confident assurance in your goodness—hope that cannot fade. Let me see you as you are, not as my temporary circumstances may tempt me to believe. I still believe that you are good.

So Much Grace

From his fullness we have all received, grace upon grace.
JOHN 1:16 NRSV

In the never-ending flow of love's mercy-tide, you are being washed new over and over again. There is more grace than there are opportunities for failure. Do not get sidetracked by your own dissatisfaction—with yourself, with others, or with God. Every moment is the chance for a fresh start.

God's love is not finite. It isn't something that can be measured. It is limitless, always flowing freely, like a rushing river whose source is pure love. Stand under the waterfall of his kindness today and let your worries and failures be washed away in its cleansing flow. There is so much grace for you!

Gracious God, I stand under your abundant tide of compassion today. Wash me afresh in your Spirit's renewal. I know that I will be better for it. What a wonderful mystery that you are full of abundance at all times. I'm so thankful to be yours.

Come Again

My life's strength melts away with grief and sadness;
come strengthen me and encourage me with your words.
PSALM 119:28 TPT

In the deluge of overwhelming sorrow, there is no amount of self-motivation that can bring relief. But there is one who holds us in comfort, offering strength for frailty and consolation for our grief. He is the breath of life, the master restorer, the only wise God.

When we have nothing left, no answers for the questions floating just under the surface, there is only one place to turn to for real relief. When we invite God to raise our awareness to the reality of his nearness, we will find hope where a moment before there was none. As we tune our hearts to his voice, we will hear the words of life he is already speaking over us.

Ever-Present God, let me hear your voice and sense your nearness once again. You are the only deep relief I have in the midst of my distress. Fill me with your words of life and let my heart take courage as you reveal your goodness even in this.

Learning to Rest

For God alone, O my soul, wait in silence,
for my hope is from him.
PSALM 62:5 ESV

There is no shame in admitting that you need more time to rest in this season. Don't keep pushing yourself to the brink. Instead, know that there is grace for you to take a step back. Loss does this well: it strips away the unnecessary so you clearly see what matters to you and what needs not be a priority right now.

Take the time to rest; sleep when you can, spend time with those who know and love you well, and let out every emotion that rises in you. You may need more time alone than you or your loved ones are accustomed to. And that is okay. There is beauty in the waiting. Recovery happens in rest. Let yourself become acquainted with the quiet places. God will speak to you there.

Loving Father, I need your help to lay down the guilt of having less margin in this season. I don't want to disappoint others, but I know that I need to prioritize rest as my whole being grieves. Give me grace to know you in the quiet places. Renew me, Lord.

Rooted in Goodness

I would have despaired unless I had believed
that I would see the goodness of the Lord
in the land of the living.

PSALM 27:13 NASB

In the desperation of loss that looks for any hints of goodness, it can feel like we're grasping at straws. Thankfully, our God is always working, sometimes under the surface while at other times clearly in our view. We have not reached the end of his faithfulness or the limits of his lovingkindness, for there are none.

We can take hope, even if it simply feels like the refusal to despair, that we will continue to see the goodness of the Lord in this life. His mercy is weaving every part of our stories into a beautiful tapestry of redemption. We will one day see clearly that the fingerprints of his loyal love are all over our lives. Take hope.

Good God, let me catch a glimpse of your goodness at work in my life today. I know that I can trust you, for you never fail. Give my heart courage as I continually cling to you in faith, believing for a better tomorrow.

Unload the Burdens

"Come to me, all you who are weary and burdened,
and I will give you rest.
Take my yoke upon you and learn from me,
for I am gentle and humble in heart,
and you will find rest for your souls."

MATTHEW 11:28-29 NIV

Will you lay your heavy burdens at the feet of Jesus today? He is waiting with kindness in his countenance and endless strength to support you. There is no need to keep crawling along on your own waning resources. He has fresh mercy to feed your soul today. He has new grace to give you.

What areas of your life feel especially overwhelming? Invite God's able hand to move on your behalf and bind your heart to his. As you partner with him, he will do all the heavy lifting. Rest now in the conviction that he will take care of you. You don't need to shoulder any worry. Let him lift the heaviness that you can't seem to shake. He is able.

Mighty God, I partner with you today. I offer you all of my heaviness and the concerns that keep mounting on each other. I depend on your strength and power to move in my life. Let my soul know true rest today.

Even More

God gives us even more grace, as the Scripture says,
"God is against the proud, but he gives grace to the humble."
JAMES 4:6 NCV

When loss steals our joy, and we cannot imagine ever feeling okay again, even then we are not alone. We are enfolded by grace, and compassion is our constant covering. We must not let our hearts despair in thinking that we have depleted God's kindness. That's not possible!

Today, there is more grace to carry us through as well as to empower us to live. When we realize our need, God is ready to infuse us with his endless mercy. In our humility, God meets us with his generous mercy. There is an abundance available to us right here and now. It's as simple as inviting him into this moment.

Gracious King, you are the one I depend upon today. I have no strength left of my own. I have nothing to offer you but myself, and that doesn't feel like much. Pour into me today with the mercy of your Spirit. Be near.

Positioned for Rescue

I'm exhausted! My life is spent with sorrow,
my years with sighing and sadness.
Because of all these troubles,
I have no more strength.
My inner being is so weak and frail.

PSALM 31:10 TPT

In your weakest moments, you have not failed God. In the frailty of your humanity, you have not disappointed him. When the only cry of your heart is a desperate plea for relief, God your Redeemer is at hand. He will not leave you to waste away in your pain. He has not abandoned you.

When you have no more strength to even lift your head, God will be the one to lift it. He will not let you be taken out by the suffering of your soul. He is here with resurrection life, breathing his love into your being. He will pull you out of the pit of despair and place your feet in a wide-open space. You *will* dance again.

Savior, I need you more than I can say. I have run out of words to express my deep need. Rescue me from the overwhelming darkness I feel! Come quickly, Lord.

Ask Again

Oh that I might have my request,
and that God would fulfill my hope.
JOB 6:8 ESV

Do not let your disappointment turn to defeat. Cry out to God as many times as it takes. He does not tire of your requests; he surely hears each one. Don't censor yourself with your Maker. He already knows you, but it's just as important that you build the connection of real relationship on your end.

God does not want a superficial, perfect version of you. He just wants you. Let him into the process of your pain. There's no use in pretending that you have it all together. Let him love you, just as you are in this moment, and don't hold back your requests even if they are the same as yesterday. He does not grow weary of the offering of the real you. You can be sure of this: he will not let you down in the end.

God, I cry out to you from the depths of my soul. Here I am, all of me. I won't be afraid to show you the vulnerable places of my heart. I will not stop asking you to meet me in the mess of my jumbled emotions. Draw near, Lord, even now.

My Sustainer

*Preserve me, O God,
for in you I put my trust.*
PSALM 16:1 NKJV

When sorrow is a stormy gale, upsetting your inner world, God is the same unchanging one. His steadfast love is the anchor that holds you in place. His constant compassion is the shelter that covers you. He will sustain you in the fiercest storm. He will keep you safe.

Though storms shake what can be shaken, there is a foundation that cannot be moved. God will not let you be lost to the winds of regret. His love is strong and able, and it is the rock upon which you stand. Even when you cannot stand, it is the bed you lay upon. It will never be destroyed.

Sustainer, I trust that even when I cannot see you, you are with me. I believe that you will not let the grief I bear be the end of me. Though I struggle to find it, I trust that I will see your goodness as clear as day in my life again. Keep me close and revive my weary heart!

He Can Take It

*Cast all your anxiety on him
because he cares for you.*
1 PETER 5:7 NRSV

The presence of anxiety does nothing to change your identity as God's chosen child. Just as a good parent invites all of their child's emotions, so it is the same with your good Father. He has endless wisdom to handle all of life's problems. Why carry the heaviness of your fretful thoughts when you have a wise and patient counselor available?

Let today be the day you choose to lay out all your fears before God. They are not too much for him to bear, and they certainly won't overwhelm him. Cast all your anxiety on him because he cares for you. Let him be your help.

Father, I lay out all of my weighty worry and the angst within my soul plainly before you. Here, you can have it all. Will you speak truth over me today? Fill my mind with your insights that bring peace and flood my heart with your kindness. I know that you see things more clearly than I do, and I trust your perspective.

Help Is Right Here

From the depths of despair, O LORD,
I call for your help.
PSALM 130:1 NLT

There is no disappointment so great that it displaces the reality of God's love. Though you may feel disheartened and discouraged, God has not changed. He has not pulled away from you. He is abundant in mercy in every moment. He is generous with his grace—just a breath away.

What if today you took God at his word? What if you believed that he would help you in whatever way you need? What difference would that make to your requests? Would you ask bigger, bolder prayers? Lay the fear aside and let your heart lead the way to the throne of the miracle maker.

Lord, I am laying aside my small thinking today and inviting you into the bigness of my loss. I know that you are larger than my discontent. I believe you will provide for me in ways that astound me. I am banking on your Word that says you are better than I can ever imagine.

No Need to Despair

"Don't worry, because I am with you.
Don't be afraid, because I am your God.
I will make you strong and will help you;
I will support you with my right hand that saves you."
ISAIAH 41:10 NCV

With God at our side, there is no reason to give over to worry. We need not abandon ourselves to the distress of our current situations with the mighty Savior as our help. No matter what we face, God's power is stronger. His love cannot be overcome though we can be overwhelmed by the liquid love of his presence.

When the voice of despair sounds convincing, may we hear the whisper of God that breaks through with truth. Every Word of God is life-giving. His Word gives strength to the weak and clear perspective to the confused mind. His Word will never strip you of hope; rather, it breathes courage to the weary heart. Which voice will you believe today?

God my help, speak your words of life over me again. I want to know your perspective which is so much broader than my limited scope. I don't want to be lost to despair. Fill me with the courage that your living Word brings.

Radiant Hope

The Lord alone is our radiant hope
and we trust in him with all our hearts.
His wrap-around presence will strengthen us.
PSALM 33:22 TPT

God has gone to war on your behalf, and he is already victorious. When Jesus rose from the dead and ascended to the right hand of his Father in heaven, all power of death was broken once and for all. He broke the chains of sin that would keep you stuck in cycles of destruction. You are free.

Beloved, even in times of great grief, nothing can change what God has already done. You are his, and you are alive in the freedom of his forever kingdom. Trust him even when you are overcome with sorrow. He will take the tears that you weep and use them to water the seeds of his kingdom; just you wait and see. Lean back now in the loving embrace of your Father.

Dearest Father, I am undone at the thought that you could use even the most painful experiences of my life for your glory. Do what only you can do. You are my hope, and I put all my confidence in you. Here's my heart, Lord; it is yours!

Love Pours In

Hope does not put us to shame,
because God's love has been poured into our hearts
through the Holy Spirit who has been given to us.

ROMANS 5:5 ESV

Does your heart feel depleted today? Or do you feel a glimmer of hope where before there was just despair? No matter the state of your heart, the Spirit of God is ready to pour more love into you today. The river of God's mercy is always flowing; it's never stagnant. As long as it is called "today," there is fresh mercy for you to receive.

There is more revelation available to you, so don't be afraid to ask for greater measure. There is no lack in God's love; there is an overflowing abundance. Will you invite God to pour more of his great love into your heart today? The Holy Spirit is always close; there's no need to go looking for pure affection. It is already yours, here and now.

Merciful One, I long for a fresh taste of your mercy today. Would you meet me with your goodness? I long for a new revelation of your love. Pour into me as I open my heart wider to you until I am consumed by the glory of your presence within me.

Limitless Love

Your lovingkindness, O Lord, extends to the heavens,
Your faithfulness reaches to the skies.

PSALM 36:5 NASB

Do not worry; you have not reached the end of God's faithfulness. He is not done writing your story, and every promise he has made he will follow through on. Will you shift your gaze from your disappointment to his vow of unending love today?

As you consider the expanse of God's loyal love, do not be discouraged by the limits of your own. He is your source; let him fill you up until you are brimming with the wonder of his ways. He will never fall short of his Word. Align your mind with his nature, remembering how good he has been. He is still good and he always will be.

Good God, I need a fresh touch of your mercy that awakens my heart to hope once again. I cannot conjure up awe on my own. Let me see the glory of your ways clearly today. I am ready for a new revelation of the greatness of your love.

Always Good

The LORD is good to those whose hope is in him,
to the one who seeks him.

LAMENTATIONS 3:25 NIV

When we are in the middle of a dark night, it can be difficult to hope for a new day's coming. Yet it will dawn all the same. In our souls we wrestle with the reality that life won't be the same after this. It won't. When day breaks, we will see that there is new fruit growing that we have not known before this. Though it is different, it will be sweet.

God is always good. He does not replace our shattered dreams with cheap substitutions. He is so much better than that. There will be a new way of life that is much deeper than what we had experienced before. Where pain digs a deep well within us, God uses it to expand our capacity for love and understanding. You will see that even in deep suffering, God plants seeds of redemption.

Lord, I have to believe that you will bring me through this time of deep sorrow with consolation. Would you give me a glimpse of the goodness that is coming so I may taste hope again? Meet me here in the midst of my grief.

New Life Coming

To all who mourn in Israel,
he will give a crown of beauty for ashes,
a joyous blessing instead of mourning,
festive praise instead of despair.
In their righteousness, they will be like great oaks
that the Lord has planted for his own glory.

ISAIAH 61:3 NLT

As surely as the sun rises each morning in the east and sets each evening in the west, so God's redemption is just as dependable. When we look and see ashes where there once stood a vibrant life, we can be sure that God will bring beauty. When our days begin and end with racking sobs of deep grief, we can know that God's comfort will not simply settle us. The fruit of the seeds of sorrow will be joy.

Your roots are growing deeper in the love of God, even now. Though the growing pains are sharp, the resulting expansion of new life will be so much greater than you can imagine. Trust the gardener of your heart to tend to you. He is gentle and his skill is unmatched.

Refiner, I rest in the knowledge of your nearness today. You have not left me to waste away in my grief. I believe that I will see your goodness again as clear as day; everything you put your hand to is marked by your glory. I trust that this season will be no different.

Everything I Need

"The Lord is my portion," says my soul,
"therefore I will hope in him."
LAMENTATIONS 3:24 ESV

We will never find the satisfaction of what we need outside of what we already have access to right now. Our God meets with us in the depths of our souls, filling us with his Spirit that brings life. He has already made provision for every need we have. There's no reason to fear that we will go without.

When was the last time you were confident of God's present goodness? When was the last time you tasted his sweet kindness in your life? He has not changed. What a wonder that he doesn't change his faithfulness to match our faith. He is the same, yesterday, today, and forever. He is your plentiful portion.

Lord, may my soul sing that you are my portion no matter what I am facing. I want to know the confidence that I once did. Revive my weary heart in the life-giving presence of your perfect peace. I trust you to do in me what only you can. Don't let me down.

Hope Is Here

I rise before dawn and cry for help;
I put my hope in your words.
PSALM 119:147 NRSV

In the moments when waking means the harsh realities of pain come rushing in, it can feel impossible to settle your mind. When awareness feels like a gut punch, over and over again, cry out to your God. He is your help. Your weakness does not define his willingness to reach out. He is always with you, and there is no need to hold back when he is already holding you.

When sleep eludes you, know that the comforter is near. He wraps you up in the warmth of his affection. Would a mother ignore the cries of her frantic child? No, and God will never ignore your cries. His peace will settle you without need for you to even articulate what you are feeling. In the depths of your pain, his deeper love covers you.

God, my only hope, when I have no words to describe the agony of my heartbreak, meet me with the tangible nearness of your presence. I need your comfort more than I can say.

Love Covers Everything

He has brought me to his banquet hall,
And his banner over me is love.
SONG OF SOLOMON 2:4 NASB

Your hunger does not dictate the abundance of what is available to you. If you can only eat bread because of the state you're in, there is no shame in that. But know that when you are ready to ingest more, there is a feast set out before you. In the banqueting hall of your great God and King, you always have a seat at the table.

In every season, love covers you. God does not look at you through eyes of disappointment but of fierce affection and devotion. However you feel about yourself, life, or even God today, it does not change the fact that the banner of God's love covers you. It always will.

Great King, I trust that your love is more than enough for me. I lay down the disappointment I feel, especially in myself, and let your kingdom reality overtake my own. Thank you for the abundance of your goodness that is present with me in every moment.

February

Look to the LORD and his strength;

seek his face always.

1 CHRONICLES 16:11 NIV

He Sees Me

He will not ignore forever all the needs of the poor,
for those in need shall not always be crushed.
Their hopes shall be fulfilled, for God sees it all!
PSALM 9:18 TPT

Take heart today, for your God and deliverer sees you. He has his attentive eye on every change in posture, every crease of your forehead. He knows just what you need, and he will surely provide it. He will not let this pain crush the life out of you. You are his beloved child, and he is here with comfort and relief.

Let your soul find rest today in the knowledge that your good Father does not miss a single detail of your life. He knows every challenge you face, and he has promised to provide for you. He has not left you as an orphan, begging for scraps to simply survive. He has lovingkindness for you today. You will taste the goodness of your God as his abundant mercy touches your life with power and provision.

Dearest Father, you are my sustenance, and your Word is my bread. I need you to do what only you can in my life. Your miracle-working resurrection power is my hope!

Never-ending Help

*Do not worry about anything,
but pray and ask God for everything you need,
always giving thanks.*

PHILIPPIANS 4:6 NCV

When worries weigh down your already overtired mind, will you let the peace of God lead you into sweet surrender once again? God's powerful love is already working in your life to produce kingdom fruit. His purposes for you have not changed. Take a moment and remember his faithfulness. Look back on the wonder of his provision in seasons past.

God is infinitely consistent. His kindness never wavers. His intentions do not change with the shifting seasons. Trust him today as you reflect on his magnanimous character. There's no need to keep a running list of possible outcomes playing out in your mind when your life is tethered to the one who sees the end from the beginning. He has all the wisdom you need and you can depend on him.

Constant One, I surrender my worry to you again today. My soul is already weary, and the fears are sapping me of any strength I could have conjured on my own. Lead me in your love and prove faithful as I rely on you.

Everlasting Life

These things I have written to you who believe in the name of the Son of God, that you may know that you have eternal life, and that you may continue to believe in the name of the Son of God.

1 JOHN 5:13 NKJV

When death knocks on our doorstep, we cannot help but reel from its effects. But we are joined to one who is not bound by expiration dates or ends of any kind. He is eternal. In him, we find the life we long for, and what's more, we have everlasting life.

Though the world as we know it will surely pass away, the coming reign of God's glorious kingdom will supersede our expectations of goodness. There will be no more weeping and no more pain. Sorrow will be but a distant memory. Though we grieve now—and oh how we grieve!—there is coming a day and age when the glory of our King will be as clear as the sun shining in a cloudless sky. And his light will never darken.

Holy God, I long for the day when sorrow and suffering are but a memory. I feel the sting of loss so acutely, and I know that you're not asking me to pretend it's not there. Let my heart fill with hope today as I remember that these temporary troubles will pale in comparison to what awaits me in eternity. I cannot wait for the sweet reunions that I will have!

Met By Mercy

*In him and through faith in him we may approach God
with freedom and confidence.*

EPHESIANS 3:12 NIV

What do you need today? Your gracious God is here with mercy,
flowing from his pure heart directly over your life. You don't have to
go searching for his goodness in the far reaches of the world. He is
present with you now. He is full of abundant love.

There is no lack too great that he cannot flood it with his kindness.
You are the recipient of his undying affection; don't fight it today.
You are met by the benevolence of his overflowing compassion
every time you turn your attention toward him. Let the grace of his
Spirit empower you today. He is so very close!

Merciful Father, I need you more than I can express. Though my
heart may wane in belief when the weight of the world presses
me down, I will not stop calling out to you. Meet me today
with your mercy.

Not to Worry

Do not throw away your confidence,
which has a great reward.
HEBREWS 10:35 NCV

When we are caught up in the waves of sorrow, it can be hard to find our bearings. What are our hearts anchored to in times of testing? When we have no strength left of our own, what is the foundation that we fall upon? Let it be the faithfulness of our God and King. He never fails.

We will not be caught in the riptide of worry when we fasten the life vest of faith around us. And even if we were to go under for a moment, our lifesaver would never let us drown. Our Savior's grip is strong and sure. He will lift us out of the turbulent waters of anguish and bring us to the shores of his peace.

Savior, I give you all of my concerns and anxieties. I'm so thankful that you don't require perfection. Keep me connected to your peace today, so I feel the weight of your nearness. Don't let me go.

Calmed by Comfort

When anxiety was great within me,
your consolation brought me joy.
PSALM 94:19 NIV

Do not let your fears convince you that there is no solace here for you. As long as you are drawing breath, the Spirit of comfort is near. Take a moment right now, before you do anything else, and let the presence of God both surround and fill you.

Let the anxieties of your mind calm as you focus your attention on the breath that moves in and out of your nostrils. Just as easily as air moves in and out, so the Spirit moves as effortlessly. With each inhalation, breathe in the conscious awareness of the Spirit with you now. With each exhalation, push out lingering fear. His perfect love is with you in overflowing measure. It is as accessible as the air around you.

Comforter, as I focus my attention on you, bring peace to my mind and heart. Flood my senses with your very present perfect peace. I yield my thoughts to you; align my heart in your love again.

Tide of Love

Let your steadfast love become my comfort
according to your promise to your servant.
PSALM 119:76 NRSV

The lavish love of God is loyal. It is the safeguard of your spirit, keeping you wrapped up in the peace of God's expansive heart. When you have nothing to offer but your weakest "yes," God meets you with the intensity of his never-ending kindness.

Do not be discouraged by your struggle. Don't let the trials you walk through become the narrative by which you experience the world. You are in the great river of God's love; his tide will bring you to where you need to go. Lean back and let his mercy carry you as you rest in him.

Loving God, I don't want to frantically kick my way out of the tides of your grace unsure of whether you will take care of me or not. Settle my heart with your peace as I hand you the reins of my life. Thank you for the reminder that I am not alone and I do not need to be in control. You lead so much better than I ever could.

All I Need

God will never give you the spirit of fear,
but the Holy Spirit who gives you
mighty power, love, and self-control.
1 TIMOTHY 1:7 TPT

Some days, the demands of present needs and unsure tomorrows threaten to overwhelm even the soundest mind. In these times, it is a good practice to slow down and look at the bigger picture. Where has God met you in uncertainty before? How has he provided for you when you could not see a way out of your circumstances?

God is more faithful than the rising sun. His mercies are new every morning. Where there is fear, look at the root of it. What has you worried today? Tell him about it. Offer God your anxieties and he will give you his peace. You already have the Holy Spirit within you—an endless resource of power, love, and self-control. Surrender your fears to him and take hold of what is already yours.

Perfect Provider, I had forgotten how trustworthy you are. I bind my heart to yours in trust, knowing that you never deal in fear or angst. I offer you all that has kept me distracted from your faithfulness and I receive your forgiving and expansive perspective.

Rooted in God's Kingdom

He will be strong, like a tree planted near water
that sends its roots by a stream.
It is not afraid when the days are hot;
its leaves are always green.
It does not worry in a year when no rain comes;
it always produces fruit.

JEREMIAH 17:8 NCV

With your heart surrendered to the King of kings, your life is planted in his higher kingdom. His ways are better and his intentions purer than any you have ever known. There is no need to worry about drought or whether you will have enough to get through. Even in times of extreme pressure, your life will produce the fruit of his Spirit that is alive in you.

You are stronger than you know, for your strength is not your own. God's mighty mercy is your source; your roots go deep in his life-giving love. Though surely the winds of testing come, you have access to an endless supply of grace under the surface. Don't fear and do not give up. Your life bears the fragrance of Spirit fruit even now.

Great God, I am so thankful for the reminder that you remain the source of all the power I will ever need. If I were relying on my own strength, I would have already failed. Give me eyes to see where your goodness is at work even now in the midst of mourning.

Not Done Yet

Rejoice in hope,
be patient in tribulation,
be constant in prayer.
ROMANS 12:12 ESV

Though the experience of suffering is inescapable in this life, God's great grace is far more persistent. He is not finished working his astonishingly good redemption work in you. Rejoice in hope, for this is not the end. You will taste the sweet fruit of joy again.

Be patient in the process of your pain, knowing that God will use this to refine your heart in the purifying fires of his love. Though weeping may last for a season, the dawn will break and you will see that he has been with you all along, sowing seeds of mercy along your path. Finally, be constant in prayer, turning your attention to him every time you think of it.

Faithful One, I turn to you again today, arms wide open to receive your grace. I fix my eyes on you, the one who called me in the first place. Do not leave me in my hour of need. Strengthen and uphold me.

Led by Love

"I will bring the blind by a way they did not know;
I will lead them in paths they have not known.
I will make darkness light before them, and crooked places straight.
These things will I do for them and not forsake them."

ISAIAH 42:16 NKJV

In the deepest valley, you are being led by love. In the blackest night, mercy's hand is holding yours. There is nowhere you could find yourself in this life—no circumstance, no suffering, no situation—that is outside of God's gracious grip. When you feel surrounded by the oppressive darkness of doubt, the Holy Spirit is there to guide you in the light of truth.

Let your heart find rest in the knowledge that God is your guide. The one who has all wisdom, endless insight, and who sees the end from the beginning is the one whose hand holds your own. He will settle the storm of your raging thoughts with his peace. He is with you.

Merciful God, bring refreshment to my soul today as I meditate on your Word. Fill me with peace as I trust you with the unknowns of my future. I need your Spirit's comfort and guidance. Keep leading me in your love, Lord, all the days of my life.

Perfect Father

*You did not receive a spirit of slavery to fall back into fear,
but you have received a spirit of adoption.
When we cry, "Abba! Father!"
it is that very Spirit bearing witness with our spirit
that we are children of God.*

ROMANS 8:15-16 NRSV

As children of God, we have been given the same inheritance that all of his beloved benefit from. There is unending mercy, unfailing love, and a storehouse of wisdom through the Holy Spirit who lives, moves, and breathes within us. There is so much more available than we could possibly imagine.

Fear is not our portion. Rather, when we feel the grip of fear's tentacles wrapping around our hearts, let us cry out to our Father. He is our defender and our advocate. May we place all our trust in him as he fights for us. We can never outrun the tidal wave of his love. Fear stands no chance against it.

Abba, you are my perfect Father. I can trust you with everything. I will not let the anxiety of the unknown disturb my confidence in you as my provider. When I forget how great you are, lead me back to you in love. I want to rest in trust today. I choose to put my faith in your capable hands.

Daybreak Is Coming

Do it again! Those Yahweh has set free will return to Zion
and come celebrating with songs of joy!
They will be crowned with never-ending joy!
Gladness and joy will overwhelm them;
despair and depression will disappear!
ISAIAH 51:11 TPT

The cycles of life do not include an endless night. Even when you've forgotten what the light of day feels like in your soul, you can be sure that the dawn of revelation is coming. Gladness and joy, though they may feel like distant memories, will be tangible once more. The heaviness of sorrow will lift. This is not the end.

Can you entertain the possibility of palpable goodness today? Even if it's an act of imagination, let your heart hope for more. The Redeemer will set you free to live unencumbered by despair. He will lead you out with songs of joy into a brighter day. He will not fail you. This moment in your life is not the end of his promises. There is more to come, and it will be full of his goodness.

Yahweh, you are the hope my heart clings to in the darkest night I've ever known. I am desperate for the relief of your tangible goodness. Come again. Let my heart stay burrowed in yours through it all. Holy Spirit, surround me with your life-giving love again today.

Satisfied Hope

I hope in You, O Lord;
You will answer, O Lord my God.
Psalm 38:15 NASB

When hope feels like a whisper instead of a shout, it holds the same kind of power. Will you let God speak his words of hope over your shattered dreams and broken heart today? He has so much life for you yet. Though your confidence wanes, his never wavers. You can trust his Word. You can trust his heart.

Where do your hopes lie? Are they in your own abilities? Are they in some far-off dream? Or do they feel like a luxury of the past—perhaps of youthful innocence? Rest assured, when your hope is found in God, it will never be disappointed. Will you let him breathe fresh courage into your heart today?

Lord, even when I struggle to believe that you will answer me, I trust that your faithfulness is not dependent on my own faith. You are far better than that. Fill me with your Spirit's wind today, blowing away the cobwebs of doubt and disappointment.

Thread of Trust

Blessed is he whose help is the God of Jacob,
whose hope is in the LORD his God.
PSALM 146:5 ESV

Let your heart be bound to God with the thread of trust. He will never stop coming through for you. No matter the trial you face, he is your advocate and your help in every single one. Why not trust him with the small details as well as the insurmountable mountains? He can handle them all; he never turns down a chance to partner with his beloved ones.

What looks impossible to you today? Invite God to show up and show off for you. He surely will. Is it wisdom that you are looking for? He's got it in abundance. Is it creativity? He's the source of it. Is it peace? He breathes it. Let your heart be encouraged by his faithfulness, for he has not changed. There's so much more available.

God of Jacob, I trust you to help me through all of the questions. I depend on your help to move the mountains that stand in my way. I look to you, offering you access to every part of my life. Do what only you can do.

Tapestry of Goodness

If we hope for what we do not see,
we eagerly wait for it with perseverance.
ROMANS 8:25 NKJV

Though days grow long, even as weeks fly by, there is a constant through it all. God's loyal love weaves a tapestry of his goodness through every season our souls encounter. In the midst of heavy grief and deep, deep sorrow, it can be hard to see any beauty. But that doesn't mean that it isn't present.

When we fix our eyes on the promised goodness of God, our souls stir with hunger. At times it feels desperate and other times it may just be a thought, but the desire remains through it all. We must know his goodness. We must know that suffering isn't wasted. Let us persevere in hope, not giving up when the road is rough. He will come through. He will do it.

Faithful One, give my heart strength to believe that you are not finished with me yet. Breathe hope into my soul where there is so much grief and sorrow. Even just a glimmer will lighten the load. I have placed all my bets on you; don't fail me, God!

Indescribable Bounty

Return to your stronghold, O prisoners of hope;
today I declare that I will restore to you double.
ZECHARIAH 9:12 NRSV

In the kingdom of God when restoration rebuilds, it does not simply meet the standards of what once was. There is always increase; God redeems what was lost and builds even more into it. There is indescribable bounty and beauty in the restoration work of Jesus.

If you feel burdened down by the gaping hole that loss has left behind, may you find courage in this. God always gives more than we've yet experienced. He does not withhold goodness from his children. He sows seeds that multiply as they grow. When you taste the fruit of this season, though you may expect bitterness, it will be sweet. Take hope!

Restorer, today I dare to hope that the suffering I am experiencing will yield fruit in the future that is lasting and sweet. You know how desperately I want to believe that there is better to come. Whisper your words of hope over my heart as I imagine what is possible with you.

Steadfast Presence

*You will keep in perfect peace
those whose minds are steadfast,
because they trust in you.*

ISAIAH 26:3 NIV

We cannot control the inevitable change of seasons or the furious storms that rip apart our comfort. We have no say over whether suffering will reach our doorsteps. There is nothing we can do to change the fact that testing will come. God did not promise us perfect lives; he never said that it would be easy.

He did, however, promise us his steadfast presence. He promised perfect peace. Will we turn our attention to his loyal love when the winds pick up, or will we let anxieties about the unknown flood our senses? Every moment is a new opportunity to choose trust. God will never change his ways. He is perfect in love. He never worries; he has no need. Let us join our hearts to his today.

Prince of Peace, I bind my heart to yours in trust today. I know that you see everything clearly though I can't seem to see what is right in front of me. When my world is spinning, you never move. I fix my eyes on you again, Unchanging One. Bring peace to my mind and calm to my heart.

Humanity of Heart

How long must I worry and feel sad in my heart all day?
How long will my enemy win over me?
PSALM 13:2 NCV

When you are discouraged by the waves of emotions that crash over you, there is no need to add shame to the mix. Look at the psalms. They reveal the humanity of hearts longing to know God. David did not only sing songs that reflected his victory and confidence. There are as many psalms that reflect the tension of suffering in his life.

When did perfection become the goal? When did ease in life become a marker of God's favor? Pour out your true heart before God today. He doesn't want your dressed-up faith. He wants your vulnerability. He wants your honesty. Be courageous and say what's really hidden in your heart today. He can handle every bit of it.

God, though I've been trying to present my best to you even in suffering, I recognize that it's not what you require of me. Meet me here and now as I give you my honesty.

Undeterred Constant

*Jesus Christ is the same
yesterday and today and forever.*
HEBREWS 13:3 NASB

When life takes its turns and unpleasant surprises catch us off guard, it can be difficult to believe that there are things that will remain unshakeable. When we feel tossed by the winds of uncertainty, let us look to our constant. His mercy is immovable.

Jesus, the one who was and is and is still to come, is the same throughout the ages. His love does not waver, nor does it redirect away from us in times of shifting. His love washes over our lives in undeterred measure in every moment. Right now, we are as wrapped up in his mercy as we ever were or will be. His intentions have not changed. He will turn every empty plot into a garden of his glory.

Jesus, I fix my attention on you today—the one who never changes in constant compassion. I quiet the distractions of my mind and set my heart on your steady purposes. Fill me with fresh revelation of your constancy so I may hold fast to faith.

Room to Feel

> *As I thought of you I moaned, "God, where are you?"*
> *I'm overwhelmed with despair as I wait for your help to arrive.*
> PSALM 77:3 TPT

Though the demands of life do not let up, there is no need to busy yourself trying to meet them all. When the waves of sorrow come, it's okay to slow down. There's no reason to push through the pain to check menial tasks off your to-do list. You can live life and still allow yourself room to feel the depths of your emotions.

Will you allow God to meet you in the place of your deep need today? Here in this moment is an opportunity for you to invite him in again. He will not leave you to despair. He will not ignore your cries for help. Reach out, and you will find that he is closer than you realized.

God, where are you now? I need you to meet me in the depth of my sorrow. Speak your words of life over me, and I will live! Tune my heart to your voice, to the songs of deliverance that you are singing over me even now. I am waiting.

Constant Companion

Surely your goodness and love will be with me all my life,
and I will live in the house of the LORD forever.
PSALM 23:6 NCV

The Lord your God is more dependable than the most attentive mother. He sticks closer than a brother. He is wiser than an intuitive counselor. He is your holy help, your constant support, and a faithful friend. Whether you feel surrounded by the love of those around you or you feel alone in your grief, you can be sure that God's compassion is close. His comfort is at hand.

Do a quick check-in today. How are you feeling toward God? Be honest. Let this look inward take you to the place of fellowship between you and the Holy Spirit. Invite the Comforter to lead you in love. You can trust his guidance. He will not lead you astray.

Constant Friend, thank you for never leaving me. I want to know the close fellowship of your Holy Spirit again today. I need you to guide me in your goodness, for I would certainly lose my way without you. I take your hand in mine. Lead me on.

Pure Affection

Praise be to the God and Father of our Lord Jesus Christ,
the Father of compassion and the God of all comfort.
2 CORINTHIANS 1:3 NIV

Today, what would it be like to find yourself in the presence and embrace of one who knows and loves you completely? One who cannot be talked out of their affection by your protests of unworthiness? The Father of compassion has known you for your whole life. He is not offended by the state of your heart, and he is not disappointed in you.

The Father is full of pure affection for you. If you let him, he will love you to life in his presence. Let him comfort the places that you have guarded. Let him into the most vulnerable parts of your soul, and he will take the utmost care in mending you. You can trust him.

Loving Father, I invite you into the weak and wounded places in my heart. In gentleness, will you heal me? In kindness, will you care for me? I have not known this kind of pure love before that requires nothing in return. Do what you will.

Signature of Love

Be still in the presence of the LORD,
and wait patiently for him to act.
Don't worry about evil people who prosper
or fret about their wicked schemes.

PSALM 37:7 NLT

In the depths of our discontent, God is unchanging. He has not changed his mind about his promises, and he has not suddenly abandoned love as his signature. He is kind, confident, strong, and infinitely more than we could ever imagine. We could never exaggerate his mercy.

Will we let worry preoccupy our thoughts today, or will we align our minds with the peace of Christ that surpasses our own understanding? God is not distracted, and his eye does not miss a detail. We can depend on his goodness. He is not in the business of making empty assurances; no, he is reliable in love.

God over all, I am relying on you to come through like you said you would. Give my heart grace that empowers me to courageously and confidently wait on you. Even now, Lord, fill me with your peace and surround me with your presence that brings life.

Tethered to Freedom

*The Lord is the Spirit,
and where the Spirit of the Lord is,
there is freedom.*
2 CORINTHIANS 3:17 NIV

Today, there is an openness to possibility. The Spirit of God is alive in you, and he is working in your life. You are not stuck, and you aren't without choice. God, in his power, dwells within you.

What areas of your life have you felt helpless in? What things seem insurmountable? Let them bow to the resurrection power of your God and King that works on your behalf. You have already been set free; even so, you are continually being freed from the lies that have kept you small. Let the truth of God's Word fill your heart with courage and your mind with clarity as the wild rhythms of his love plays over your life.

Holy Spirit, I offer you access to every area of my heart. I don't want to be tethered down by lies anymore. Let the truth of your Word set my feet to dancing as I celebrate liberty's ringing song over my life. Thank you for freedom!

It's Not Forever

There is hope for a tree, if it is cut down
that it will sprout again,
and that its tender shoots will not cease.
JOB 14:7 NKJV

In barren seasons, when the bounty of yesterday feels like a distant memory, we have a hope to hold onto. God is our redeemer, offering new life where old ways and dreams have died. Even as a tree is stripped bare in the winter, so we also experience times of shedding. But that is not the tree's end, and it certainly isn't ours.

Will we trust that our winter will not last forever? There is simplicity and clarity in the midst of our cleared-out seasons. This is an opportunity to remember that the pain of our present circumstances is not a sentence of doom. There is more ahead, and it is full of life. We will know the joy of blossoming spring once again. Hold onto hope.

Resurrected One, I am grateful for the reminder today that my present painful circumstances will not last forever. Just as nature shifts with seasons, so does my life. I look forward to the spring that is coming. In the meantime, will you give me eyes to see what your hand is doing in my life right now?

Without a Word

Behold, the eye of the LORD is on those who fear him,
on those who hope in his steadfast love.
PSALM 33:18 ESV

There is a feeling of loneliness in grief, even grief that is shared with loved ones. There is a deep sense of knowing that how you experience your pain is unique, and the depths of it are nearly impossible to let somebody in on. But there is one who knows it. Without a word, he understands.

Will you let God meet you in the depths of your sorrow with his comfort? He sees. He knows. He shares in it with you. Though you may feel alone in your suffering—even when surrounded by others—God encounters your deep grief with his even deeper love. You are not alone in this; you are never alone.

Comforter, I long to know your healing presence in the deepest parts of my pain. I confess that I have felt alone at times in this. Take the knowledge of your nearness from my head and move it to my heart. I want to experience true comfort today.

Confident Anticipation

You are my hope; O Lᴏʀᴅ God,
You are my confidence from my youth.

PSALM 71:5 NASB

When all is going well in life, hope seems to abound. But true hope has nothing to do with our circumstances. It is the confident anticipation of good from the provision of an even better Father. Though heartbreak robs our comfort and messes with our agendas, it can never change the nature of our all-consistent God.

God doesn't ever go back on a promise that he has made. He is true to his Word, and that is something we can depend upon. His character is not moved by the shifting ideals of the world and its systems. He is constant in unending mercy and loyal in his compassion. Whether in times of drought or in seasons of plenty, we can trust in him.

Faithful One, I confess that it has been hard for me to hold onto any hope. It is a battle in my mind to believe that I will experience deep joy in my daily life again. Today, I bind my heart to yours, believing that you are better than my circumstances. You are my only lasting hope.

March

We are confident that he hears us
whenever we ask for anything
that pleases him.

1 JOHN 5:14 NLT

Signature of Redemption

"The blind see again, the crippled walk,
[le]pers are cured, the deaf hear, the dead are raised back to life,
an[d] the poor and broken now hear of the hope of salvation!"
MATTHEW 11:5 TPT

When mercy meets creation through astounding miracles, how can we but stand in awe of God's wonder-working power? The ministry of Jesus on this earth is but a small taste of the powerful love of God that chases us down over and over again. He is full of compassion, moved by kindness in all he does.

Let our hearts align with the pure motives of God's great grace. As we look at the life of Jesus, may we brim with the hope that redemption's signature is also on our lives. He heals diseases, mends broken hearts, and makes a way where there was none. He is adept at creating solutions out of impossible situations. He is the same yesterday, today, and forever.

Unchanging One, my heart is hopeful that you will do the same kind of miracles in my life that you have in others. As long as I draw breath into my lungs, I will trust that you are not done with me. Change my life; reorder my steps if you must. Fill me with the awe of your wonderful news.

Much to Glean

*Be humble under God's powerful hand
so he will lift you up when the right time comes.*
1 PETER 5:6 NCV

When life presses you down, do not fear. The Lord your God will not let you be crushed. He will lift you up, and you will run in the light of life again. Trust his timing and know that he is present even now with sufficient grace. Even in the waiting, there is so much to glean. Stay open.

You can trust God's leadership in life even in the middle of your suffering. He will never abandon you. He always leads in love. In the shaking, he will stir you to life. You don't have to strive to get ahead; trust the guidance of your faithful God as he works all things together for your good.

Great God, lead me in your goodness. When I cannot understand what you are doing, I yield my life to your purposes. I know that you are good. I trust that you are for me. Have your way in me.

Dwelling Place

God's dwelling place is now among the people,
and he will dwell with them.
"He will wipe every tear from their eyes.
There will be no more death" or mourning or crying or pain,
for the old order of things has passed away.

REVELATION 21:3-4 NIV

There is coming a day when every tear will be wiped away and death will be just a memory. Then we will see clearly, face-to-face, and understand as completely as we are already known. Until then, we have fellowship in spirit and truth. As we await the coming of our King, he is with us now.

We catch glimpses of the glory of the coming kingdom of God in this life. As we do, may our hearts turn toward him in childlike wonder. Until God makes his physical dwelling with us, we have the indwelling of his Spirit available to us. The God of the ages breathes new life into us through the fellowship of his Spirit ministering to ours.

Holy God, I can hardly imagine what seeing you will be like. I long for the knowing, for the uncertainty to finally come to an end. Awaken me to your life today and deposit heavenly wisdom and revelation within my understanding. I just want to know that you are near and that you are here.

In His Sight

*Humble yourselves in the sight of the Lord,
and He will lift you up.*

JAMES 4:10 NKJV

Today, know that you are seen by the King of kings. You are not hidden from him. The cloud of your grief does not affect his sight; he sees you clearly. Turn your attention to him in this moment. His gaze pierces through the fog of your sorrow and burns up the mist of your disappointment with the light of his love.

Beloved, take heart. You are not lost to the sea of despair; you are tethered to the unchanging mercy-heart of God through it all. He lifts those who cannot stand on their own. He carries the weary; all you need to do is rest in his arms. Trust him to get you through. He will do it.

Loving God, I lean into your arms today. I have no strength of my own to pull myself along. Carry me through this and surround me with the confidence of your peaceful presence. I depend on you.

Destiny of Freedom

He delivered us from such a deadly peril, and he will deliver us.
On him we have set our hope that he will deliver us again.

2 CORINTHIANS 1:10 ESV

We can never exhaust the love of God. His mercy cannot be dammed up. He has delivered us out of the bondage of fear into the freedom of his kindness. His fiery love burns up anything that does not belong to his kingdom of light. He will continue to deliver us.

Wherever we feel stuck is an invitation for God's great liberation. Freedom is our destiny. We can trust him to come through. He will time and again. He will do it. When we place our bets on the faithfulness of our Great Redeemer, we will never lose.

Faithful Father, I'm so thankful that you don't ever stop delivering me from my troubles. As I align my life with yours over and over again, would you set me free in new ways? I want to walk in the joy of salvation.

Mercy Covering

You bless the righteous, O Lord;
you cover them with favor as with a shield.
PSALM 5:12 NRSV

Your life is hidden in the mercy covering of your good God. Even in the midst of the overwhelming pull of pain, God has not abandoned you. You are still his beloved, and he won't stop working on your behalf. In your struggle, don't be swayed to believe that you have somehow lost God.

The Lord promises to never leave or forsake his children. You are not an exception. He is with you. He will bring peace to the chaos and smooth out even the most tangled mess. He masterfully restores your life. As you rest in him you will see that it is true.

Lord, I have to believe that you have not left me to waste away in the wasteland of my grief. I trust that you are covering me with your great grace. Someday I will clearly see that you have been working in every detail of my life. Give me a glimpse today.

Renewed Strength

*"You were tired out by the length of your road,
Yet you did not say, 'It is hopeless.'
You found renewed strength,
Therefore you did not faint."*

ISAIAH 57:10 NASB

When the road of your suffering seems to stretch on without any end in sight, what will you do? God has so much grace for your process; he does not require perfect responses or unwavering faith in order to help you. You are his dearly loved child, and he has goodness to give you.

He is giving you strength for your weariness; lean on him. He is giving you hope for despair; let his words of life fill your heart. He is giving you his perfect peace for your racing thoughts; turn your attention toward him. Search your heart. What do you really need from him today? Ask your good Father, for he is generous with you.

My God, renew my strength as I yield my heart, my mind, and my soul to you once again. I am tired of drudging along in sorrow. Would you give me sweet relief today in your presence?

My Portion

*My people will live free from worry
in secure, quiet homes of peace.*

ISAIAH 32:18 TPT

There is a peace that surpasses all understanding. There is joy that springs from a deep well that is untouched by the shifting circumstances of life. There is a love that makes fear seem like a miniscule, insignificant thing. When was the last time you felt connected to this kind of pure peace, unhindered joy, and lavish love?

There is an abundance for you within the expansive lengths of God's heart. He has promised that worry is not the portion of his people. Will you cast all your anxiety on him today? Will you let him flood you with the awareness of his life-giving presence? What he gives is better than you could ever imagine receiving.

Generous One, what you promise sounds too good to be true. I want to know the tangible peace that you promise. I want to live in the confidence of resolute trust in your faithfulness. I must know you. If you are this good, I am desperate for a touch from you!

Endlessly Good

*To him who is able to do immeasurably
more than all we ask or imagine,
according to his power that is at work within us,
to him be glory...for ever and ever! Amen.*

EPHESIANS 3:20-21 NIV

As children of God, our lives are marked by his faithfulness. He will not let this time be any different. He has more than enough mercy to get us through. His love is as present on our darkest days as it is in our greatest celebrations. His wisdom is unparalleled, and he is never, ever at a loss for what to do.

What would it be like to let our imaginations run wild with the possibilities of his goodness? Even those imaginings would fall short of the reality of his extensive creativity. He is endlessly good, outrageously kind, and overwhelmingly thoughtful. What a meditation that is: consider his marvelous goodness today.

Glorious God, as I consider how wonderful you are, my understanding cannot hold the reality of your generosity. Fill my heart with hope as you work all things out in my life with your loyal love and marvelous mercy. I need to know your goodness.

Safe Space

The LORD also will be a refuge for the oppressed,
a refuge in times of trouble.
PSALM 9:9 NKJV

In times of trouble, we have a tower of refuge to run into. Our shelter and high place is God Almighty. He is our protector—a strong defense! He is a place of refuge at all times to those who need respite from the worries of this life. He is a place of peace to those ravaged by the wars of this world.

There is no better place to be found than in the fortress of our great God and King. He is helper to the helpless, keeping guard at all times. When the storms of this life rage, may our first response be to run into the presence of our very present help. Why let fear overtake us when we belong to the victor over every foe including the grave?

Mighty God, I run into the shelter of your presence again today. I need your covering; I know you never leave and you don't lift your hand from my life, but my confidence wavers when the storms pick up. I fix my eyes on you and remember that you hold me fast; you won't let go of me.

Path of Love

Know that wisdom is thus for your soul;
If you find it, then there will be a future,
and your hope will not be cut off.

PROVERBS 24:14 NASB

What is your mind feasting on these days? Do you find yourself consumed by fear, or are you distracted by the endless cycle of worrisome news? There is a better way. You don't have to be completely disconnected from reality in order to recognize the wisdom of God's greater way.

God sees everything clearly, and he is not swayed by rumors. He has no need, for he already knows how everything connects and how it will turn out in the end. Wouldn't you rather trust the wisdom of the one who knows it all? It is not elusive. Look into the Word and find keys to life. He has not left you to figure things out on your own. Walk on the path of his wise love, and your mind will know peace.

Wise God, I give up trying to figure out things on my own. I want to live with your wisdom as my counsel. I want to believe your Word that says that there is a future and a hope for all who call on your name. Help me to choose well the things I listen to. Wisdom, teach me.

Not Cut Off

Surely there is a future,
and your hope will not be cut off.
PROVERBS 23:18 ESV

Beloved, as long as you are breathing, you have not reached the end of God's goodness in your life. There is more. You will see that the thread of his mercy runs through even your hardest heartbreak. He has not left you to bide your time in misery until you breathe your last breath. He is here with hope, he is here with mercy, and he is here with redemption.

Even when you lay your head to rest for the final time on this earth, you can know that is not your end. There is a future that no one can steal from you. There is everlasting life that will make your temporary troubles and pain pale in comparison to its glory. Your hope will not be cut off.

Everlasting God, some days it seems like a fairy tale to believe that I will know joy again. But I want to believe it! I want to be convinced, to the core of my being, that I will see your goodness again. And I want the confidence of your coming kingdom even more.

Held Together

He's the hope that holds me and the Stronghold to shelter me,
the only God for me, and my great confidence.

PSALM 91:2 TPT

When you feel as if you are being torn apart at the seams by the intensity of your grief, you need not fear. God, your Creator and your keeper, is holding you together. He will not let the pain crush you completely. He will not let you be consumed by your sorrow.

Let the track record of God's faithfulness be your confidence. He will not let you go, and he won't let you down. The thread of his love is weaved through your life; it is stronger than the storms you face. It cannot be ripped out of your story. Let God be your hope today. He holds you fast and secure.

Loving God, I trust you to hold me together when I am falling apart. I have no strength of my own; I rely completely upon you. Don't let my hope be in vain. Bring me through this with your comfort as my support and your love as my foundation.

Living Love

We want you to know what will happen to the believers who have died so you will not grieve like people who have no hope. For since we believe that Jesus died and was raised to life again, we also believe that when Jesus returns, God will bring back with him the believers who have died.

1 THESSALONIANS 4:13–14 NLT

When death reaches our doorstep and takes from us what we have cherished, the loss is palpable. It rocks our world. It may feel as though everything has changed and nothing is sacred. But there is an unchanging one in our midst. His love never wavers, and it cannot be taken from us.

Jesus defeated death when he rose from the grave. His resurrection power still reigns today. He has given us a *living* hope. It will never pass away. If we have aligned our hearts with his vibrant love, this hope will break through the ashes of barren places in our lives. We cannot escape his power at work within us.

Resurrected One, it is your power that breaks the chains of sin and death. There is nothing that your love has left untouched. Let me see your living love at work in my life; give me eyes to see. Even when it feels as though all hope is lost, I know that I cannot lose you.

Unwavering Love

The LORD takes pleasure in those who fear him,
in those who hope in his steadfast love.
PSALM 147:11 NRSV

The love of God is a rock-steady foundation beneath your feet. Even when you stumble, if you were to fall, it is the rock of his salvation that you would fall upon. You cannot wander away from his mercy. You can't outrun his grace. It is a vast ocean and your life is but a grain of sand in its midst.

Let the hope of your heart be found in the steady love of your God that follows wherever you go. It goes before you, and it follows behind. It surrounds your life. You are completely covered by the affectionate kindness of your good Father. He sees you, he knows you, and he passionately loves you.

Good Father, I submit my heart to your lavish love once again. I am so thankful that I cannot outrun your goodness. Chase me down, if you must; I need to know you more! Overwhelm my life with the goodness that your love brings.

All Access Pass

This hope we have as an anchor of the soul,
both sure and steadfast,
and which enters the Presence behind the veil.

HEBREWS 6:19 NKJV

There is nothing that separates you from the love of God today. You have access to the presence of God right here in this moment. Will you turn your attention toward him as he lavishes his compassion on you? There is no reason to wait.

You don't have to be in the perfect frame of mind; you don't have to feel confident in your intentions or have only pleasant thoughts about God to approach him. He can handle you just as you are, and he wants you no other way. Enter into his presence with the boldness of a dearly loved child, even if you come in with pointed questions. Come as you are. You have his attention.

Father, I come to you today just as I am, no holds barred. I won't keep myself stewing in the swirl of my emotions, keeping you out of it. I trust that you will settle my heart in ways I can't on my own. In any case, here I am.

Reflected in Loss

Love bears all things,
believes all things,
hopes all things,
endures all things.
1 CORINTHIANS 13:7 ESV

Love cannot spare us from pain. The only thing that can do that is indifference, and is that truly living? The depth of your pain echoes the depth of what you poured out in love. Let your heart take solace in the depth of what you shared.

The Father of love wraps around you with the liquid mercy of his presence, holding you close. His affection is the purest you will ever find. It is patient and full of hope. Can you find courage to face the pain you feel, knowing that you are practicing laid-down-love even in this way? You are not alone.

Lord, let love be the anchor that holds me in place through the storm of grief. Help me to see the loss I feel as a reflection of the love that was present. I want to be like you—patient and kind. Help me to be this way with myself first.

Stirring of Hope

On the day I called you, you answered me.
You made me strong and brave.
PSALM 138:3 NCV

Have you ever felt like God was late? Perhaps if he had listened harder or shown up sooner, things would be better? There is no one-size-fits-all solution to life. There are so many mysteries and questions left unanswered. But that does not mean that God has forgotten you. His wisdom sees what you cannot see.

Will you continue to call out to God for help? He will provide it. Look over your walk with him; remember the ways he has shown up and shown off in your life. Can you feel it? The stirring of hope? Don't rush from this moment. Consider what he has done throughout history as well as in your own life. He will do it again, and he won't delay.

God, I see your fingerprints on my life. Though I am disappointed and full of sorrow, I trust that you will leave your mark of goodness even here in the valley of the shadow of death. Give me eyes to see and answer my cries!

Whispered Help

*It is good that one should hope and wait quietly
for the salvation of the Lord.*

LAMENTATIONS 3:26 NKJV

In the suffering of the soul, not all pain makes us shout. There is a quiet sorrow that seeps through moment to moment, like a low tone droning on unheard by most. But God hears it all. A whispered "help" is as poignant to him as one that is loudly exclaimed.

Don't worry; your help is coming. The track record of your faithful rescuer is unmatched by any other. He would not let his people waste away in the desert, and he will not let you wither in this wasteland. Let his faithfulness be your confidence today. He is still good. He is for you, and he is good.

Great Redeemer, I wait in hope today for your rescue. I trust that you won't let me be swallowed up by my sorrow. Overwhelm my fears with your great mercy. I remember your faithfulness. Come through for me again. I need you!

Detailed Gaze

I pray that the eyes of your heart may be enlightened,
so that you will know what is the hope of His calling,
what are the riches of the glory of His inheritance in the saints.

EPHESIANS 1:18 NASB

God's gaze takes in the vastness of all creation, yet he doesn't miss a detail. Not even a hair falls to the ground without him taking notice. Have you forgotten that there are no mysteries to God? He sees all with clarity. When you are looking for wisdom, why would you search the ends of the earth when you already have access to the one who knows it all?

You can never ask for too much from your God. He freely gives revelation to all who look to him. Take some time today and ask him to give you eyes to see your circumstances from his perspective. May your heart hold space for his presence as you seek clarity.

Wise God, I want to know what you see when you look at my life. I don't want to be stuck in disappointment over my own lack of understanding anymore. I make room for you, Lord. Speak to me and show me your goodness once again.

Freedom in Honesty

Your faith and love rise within you as you access all the treasures of your inheritance stored up in the heavenly realm. For the revelation of the true gospel is as real today as the day you first heard of our glorious hope, now that you have believed in the truth of the gospel.

COLOSSIANS 1:5 TPT

Today is full of fresh opportunities to access God's infinite mercy. He has not changed at all. He is not disappointed in you, whether you are full of faith in his goodness or questioning the motives of his heart. You can bank on this: your questioning does not change the solid foundation of his love.

Will you present your true self to God today, not bothering to put on the flimsy veil of who you think you should be? You will find freedom in your honesty, and he will meet you with his better word. God's wisdom is as pure and true today as it ever was or will be. Align your heart with his truth, and you will not be disenchanted.

Spirit of Wisdom, come and meet with me today. Give me revelation to see who you are and who I am to you. Here I am, with all my flaws and the mess of my intense emotions all jumbled up before you. Meet me, Lord. Untangle the lies I have believed and replace them with your truth.

Capacity Exceeded

The Lord always keeps his promises;
he is gracious in all he does.
PSALM 145:13 NLT

There is no way to measure God's faithfulness. It exceeds our capacity to calculate. He is infinitely good, magnanimously merciful, and he never, ever fails. Everything he does is with love and generosity. It is beyond our imagining, the purity of his motives. He cannot be convinced out of his compassion. Oh, what a wonder!

No claims otherwise can stop God from doing what he said he will do. He always keeps his promises. He won't stop now. We are covered by his compassion, and held fast by his love—yesterday, today, and forever. He is still faithful to his Word.

Lord, let my heart grow deeper in the conviction of your goodness. If I have any confidence in this life, let it be in your faithfulness to always come through. I believe that you are with me, you are for me, and you'll never let me go. You are my God, and I trust in you.

Steady Grasp

The Lord is good, a refuge in times of trouble.
He cares for those who trust in him.

NAHUM 1:7 NIV

If today's troubles feel like too much to bear, press into the refuge of the presence of God. Let him shelter you with the empowering comfort of his love. He cares about what you are going through. He tends to you like a mother to her sick child. He holds you close in the compassionate embrace of his Spirit.

There is nowhere that you can find yourself outside of his steady grasp of grace. Will you trust him with your heart today? He is gentle and attentive, knowing just what you need before you are even aware of it. Hide yourself in the shelter of God's life-giving love and find rest for your weary soul.

Rock of Ages, I run into the refuge of your presence today. I have no desire to pull myself up by the bootstraps and keep going in my own strength. I've run out of my meager resources. I need you. Give me rest as I give you access to every part of my life that I've been trying to control. I know you are better than I am at holding things together.

Hidden in Love

You are my hiding place;
You shall preserve me from trouble;
You shall surround me with songs of deliverance.

PSALM 32:7 NKJV

There is no shame in admitting when you have run out of resources. Just like a car needs fuel to keep going, so do you; your physical, emotional, and spiritual reservoirs need to be filled. When you find yourself dried up in any way, know that there is a place of rest that you can go to be satisfied.

Hide yourself in God's heart today and see what that does for your soul. Let his love wash over you. Any time you feel overwhelmed by the demands of your day, shift your attention to God's abundant provision that is already pouring over you. He is singing his songs of relief over you now.

Mighty God, I set my attention on your greatness today. You have everything I need, and I know I don't need to go looking for it anywhere else. I trust you today. Help me to redirect my gaze to you throughout my day. You are the vision I need to see.

Unhindered Connection

The name of the Lord is a strong tower;
the righteous runs into it and is safe.
PROVERBS 18:10 NASB

In the day of your trouble, run into the heart of God. Fill your mind with the truth of his nature and you will have an answer for every lie that tries to tempt you from trust. Write his Word upon your heart; meditate on his goodness. Remember his faithfulness. He has not changed.

Submit your thoughts to the Holy Spirit's wisdom alive within you and you will be able to discern between what is right and life-giving and what fuels fear within you. Whatever promotes unhindered connection with your good Father is worth its weight in gold. Do not be distracted by the worries that threaten your peace. Run into the safe harbor of God's expansive goodness today.

Lord, I run into your presence as I align my heart with your Word. Fill my mind with the truth of your faithfulness today, that it may be a banner of hope over my thoughts. Your ways are better than the world's, and I want to know what you say over my life.

My Caretaker

The LORD is all I need.
He takes care of me.
My share in life has been pleasant;
my part has been beautiful.

PSALM 16:5-6 NCV

Will you take a few moments today to recall the ways that God has astounded you with his goodness in past seasons? Can you pinpoint a time when you were overcome with awe and gratitude at how he came through for you? His hand of provision is not a new development in your life. If nothing comes to mind, ask the Holy Spirit for help.

God is not finished taking care of you. His mercy is plentiful for every moment that you will ever face. Your problems are not too big for him. He will keep you as he delivers you into greater freedom. Do not lose hope today. Let your fears subside in the vastness of God's faithfulness.

Good Shepherd, as I look back over my life, will you highlight your presence within it? I have tasted and seen your goodness before, but I want greater vision to see what I have not seen before. Keep leading me in love and cover me in the comfort of your embrace.

Led in Victory

The LORD your God is the one who goes with you to fight for you against your enemies to give you victory.

DEUTERONOMY 20:4 NIV

Have you been beaten down by the battle at your doorstep? Today, turn your attention to the very one who fights for you. You are not alone, and you will not be crushed by the struggle. Your mighty God goes ahead of you, leading the way. He surrounds you with the shield of his compassion. This is not your end.

There is no reason to try to fight your battles alone. God will give you victory, for he has already overcome every foe you will ever face. Take his hand, trust his timing, and rest in the confidence of his ability. He is your advocate and your defender. And he is victorious.

Lord my God, I don't want to fight anymore; my strength is depleted. But then, you never required me to advocate for myself. Will you do what only you can do? Overcome what is devastating me. You are greater. Lead me into your victory.

Entwined

Here's what I've learned through it all:
Don't give up; don't be impatient;
be entwined as one with the Lord.
Be brave and courageous, and never lose hope.
Yes, keep on waiting—for he will never disappoint you!
PSALM 27:14 TPT

Today, you are covered in the luminous light of God's love. Every moment, in the same abundance of God's heart, you have the kindness of his favor. When the waiting grows long, dig into the fruit of his faithfulness that has been stored up throughout your life. Look to the wisdom of those who have walked this path before. There is encouragement to be found!

Above all, let your heart remain tightly knit into the fabric of God's mercy. Spend time in his presence, filling up on the fresh portion of comfort he offers you. He is as good as he ever was or will be, and you have access to the overflowing abundance of his kingdom today.

Father, as I look to you today, will you wrap me tighter into your love? I need a fresh revelation from your heart. Your words of life give me courage; tune my ears to hear your voice throughout my day.

Promises Kept

Sustain me according to Your word, that I may live;
And do not let me be ashamed of my hope.
PSALM 119:116 NASB

Do not lose hope today, for your God is working on your behalf. His promises are kept according to his Word, and he never wavers in love toward you. Do you need a fresh shot of courage today? Look over the vows he has made to his people throughout the ages and see how he has followed through time and again!

Sometimes the encouragement we're looking for is found outside of our own circumstances. When was the last time you were moved by a miracle in another's life? The same God who moves on behalf of others is the one who is working in your life. He will not let you be ashamed of the confidence you put in him. He will come through for you.

Faithful One, you are the ultimate promise keeper. I don't need to remind you of what you would say you would do, but oh, how I need those reminders. Will you reveal your marvelous mercy again to me today and remind me of your assurances even if they look different than I expected?

Healing Touch

For you who fear my name,
the sun of righteousness shall rise
with healing in its wings.
MALACHI 4:2 ESV

There is no wound that cuts too deep that God cannot mend it with his healing touch. His love reaches beyond our understanding to the places we don't even know to go. He is the healer. Look at the life of Jesus and the countless times he healed those who had no hope outside of him.

What seems beyond his reach today? Rest assured, even that is within his range. Your heartache is not too much for him to mend, and your problems are not too complex for him to set straight. He is a master rebuilder, restorer, and redeemer. Will you trust him with your heart?

Healer, my prayer is simple. You are welcome into my heart and into every area of my life; heal what no one else can and deliver me from the depths of my suffering. Only you can restore me.

Part of the Scope

"In My Father's house are many mansions. I go to prepare a place for you. And if I go and prepare a place for you, I will come again and receive you to Myself; that where I am, there you may be also."
JOHN 14:2-3 NKJV

This life, with its troubles and triumphs, is only part of the scope of our existence. There is a far greater hope that we have to look forward to, a coming age that will be free from heartache, pain, and loss. Any joys that we experience here, we will experience in greater measure in the realm of God's kingdom. Though we catch glimpses of his goodness, there will be nothing to block our view from his great glory when we're living in the fullness of his light.

Whether this is a comforting reminder or a new thought, let your heart take root in wonder and hope today; hope for better, for more than you can imagine. His kingdom is without end and his goodness will never diminish.

Jesus, you are the hope of my salvation. Give my heart courage to hope in your Word today, to hope that this is not the end. Not even my best day on this earth is the end of your goodness; my worst certainly won't be. There's always so much more.

April

The earnest prayer
of a righteous person
has great power
and produces wonderful results.

JAMES 5:16 NLT

House of Mercy

A father of the fatherless and a judge for the widows,
is God in His holy habitation.
God makes a home for the lonely;
He leads out the prisoners into prosperity.

PSALM 68:5-6 NASB

Let this be the reminder you needed: God takes care of the humble, and he always welcomes the needy. Do not despise your weakness. God is in the business of giving strength to those who have run out of their own. He sets the lonely in families, and he abundantly provides for those who have nothing to offer.

You don't need to bring God what you do not have. Bring your open heart and give him access to what you do have. There is no need to hold back from him today. He will meet you with the plenty of his mercy and the generosity of his goodness. Find your home in him, and you will always have a safe place to rest.

Father, it seems that I am endlessly confronted with what I don't have. I long for more, but I don't know how to get it. Today, I give up trying to figure it out on my own, and I come to your house of mercy. Feed me with the sustenance of your living Word.

Champion Defender

He alone is my safe place;
his wrap-around presence always protects me.
For he is my champion defender;
there's no risk of failure with God.
So why would I let worry paralyze me,
even when troubles multiply around me?

PSALM 62:2 TPT

Will you let God's greatness engulf what is overwhelming you today? He is bigger than your biggest problem. He is stronger than the intimidation tactics of the enemy. His power is greater than any that man wields. He is wiser than the most prestigious minds throughout all of the ages combined.

Let God defend you today. He is more than able to set wrong things right. He turns crooked paths into roads that lead straight to his kingdom. Don't fear the unknowns of tomorrow. Rest in the confidence of your great God and King. He will not let you be crushed.

Defender of my heart, I rely on you to bring me through every trial and trouble. I don't want to be paralyzed by worry—not even for a second. Flood me with your peace as you rise to my defense. Keep me close!

Tranquility

The LORD is my shepherd, I shall not want.
He makes me lie down in green pastures;
he leads me beside still waters;
he restores my soul.
PSALM 23:1-3 NRSV

God does not impart chaos, and he is not confusing. When our minds are full of noise and we cannot decipher the feelings of our hearts, God is our place of peace. He leads us to tranquility and calms our hearts and minds in the harmony of his Spirit.

When we are burdened by the heaviness of this world and the tragedies of life, our Good Shepherd takes us by the hand and leads us beside the still waters of his mercy. He never stops restoring our souls. May we be quick to follow his lead, for he guides us with his generous grace.

Shepherd of my soul, lead me to your peaceful presence again today. I long for the refreshing waters of your living Word to wash over my mind in a fresh way. My being needs the rest you offer; I am so very tired. Guide me into your strength again.

So Very Near

You are near, Lord,
and all your commands are true.
PSALM 119:151 NIV

When the days are dark from the moment your eyes open in the morning, let your heart recall this timeless truth: God is with you. He engulfs you with the love of his presence. He is nearer than you know, closer than you could ever imagine.

When your heart is broken open and the weeping lasts from day to night, the Lord holds you; he catches every tear. Not one will be forgotten. See how his heart is moved with compassion. He cries with you, sharing the bitter cup of grief. He will not leave you to mourn alone. He will not leave you period. He is so very near.

Lord, reveal yourself to me in the darkest hours of my grief. I have known you in the celebration of my deepest joys. I must know you in the tearing open of my soul. Don't ever let me go even if I protest. I want to know your steadfast, all-encompassing love that seeps into every cell of my being.

Hurricane Force

My God is my rock. I can run to him for safety.
He is my shield and my saving strength,
my defender and my place of safety.
The LORD saves me from those who want to harm me.

2 SAMUEL 22:3 NCV

When the winds of testing come with hurricane force, we have a place of shelter to run and hide. What's more, the foundation of our lives is immoveable; the strong rock of God's faithful love cannot be shaken. When we cannot stand for fear of being blown over by the storm's gales, may we press close to the bedrock of our salvation.

Jesus is the same yesterday, today, and forever. He will not let us be swept away by the storms of this life. He overpowers what overwhelms us. Even now he has overcome every devastation with his powerful redemption. Our hearts are tethered to his by the three-strand cord of his love, and it can never be broken.

Savior, I depend on you to save me from the storm that is raging within my soul. I know that you give freedom and peace to your people, and I am waiting for my breakthrough! Open my eyes to that which has not changed—that which is lasting. Surround me with your peace.

Honorable Transparency

Don't hide yourself, Lord, when I come to find you.
You're the God of my salvation;
how can you reject your servant in anger?
You've been my only hope,
so don't forsake me now when I need you!

PSALM 27:9 TPT

Do you feel desperate to know that God is with you, that he hasn't forgotten you? Don't be afraid to be honest with your humanity; it is no mystery to God when you struggle. He will not hide himself so you cannot find him. Cry out for understanding if that is what you long for today.

Whatever it is that you need, God can provide it. Lay it all out plainly before him. Your transparency is your honor. Do not hold back today. Open up and let the light of life shine on you once again.

God of my salvation, I have so many questions. I can't pretend that I am confident in all that I wish I were. Meet me in the vulnerability of my true state today. I won't hold back; I ask that you would do the same.

Divine Love

His divine power has granted to us everything pertaining to life and godliness, through the true knowledge of Him who called us by His own glory and excellence.

2 PETER 1:3-4 NASB

We have been called by the author of love to live in the power of his kingdom come to earth. That means whenever we face trials, we have access to a greater capability than our own. He gives strength for weakness, beauty for ashes, and life for death.

Our redeemer meets us in the midst of our mess and he weaves his mercy through it until he has made something even more glorious of the remnants. There is no chaos that cannot be tamed by him. We have no need to worry about what will become of us because we are wrapped up into the greatest love story this world has known. We have everything we need in him.

Mighty God, keep your hand on my life, leading me into greater healing. I know that as my redeemer you won't leave any broken part of my heart or life untouched by your resurrection power. I long to taste your life-giving love once again. Fill me afresh today with your tangible presence.

Flags of Courage

*"I have said these things to you,
that in me you may have peace.
In the world you will have tribulation.
But take heart; I have overcome the world."*

JOHN 16:33 ESV

When our hearts are heavy with sorrow and we wonder how we got to this place, will we come back to the place of our refuge? Jesus is the lifter of burdens. He didn't promise that we would have a pain-free life; he promised that we would have peace in the midst of our troubles.

Hard truths are not always welcome. But here, in the midst of our suffering, we can find solace that God knows our pain and he shares in it. The overwhelming grief we feel is nothing compared to the victory that Jesus has in his overcoming of death. He overpowered the grave so we can stand in his victory with flags of courage waving high in our hearts. There is not one situation we face that has not been conquered by love already!

Victorious One, would you blanket me in your peace today? I want to rest in the confidence that though this weeping may continue for a season, the joy of a new day is coming. May my soul find the respite it needs in you as I turn my awareness to you, the conquering Lion of Judah.

Calm and Clarity

*"I am leaving you with a gift—peace of mind and heart.
And the peace I give is a gift the world cannot give.
So don't be troubled or afraid."*

JOHN 14:27 NLT

Can you think of the best gift you've ever received in your lifetime? Now imagine that every morning you were given a gift of equal importance. How beautifully blessed would you feel? God's gifts are like that. He is always pouring out his love offerings to us through his Spirit. If we will take the time to build the fellowship we freely have, we will experience the awareness of his goodness in our midst.

Today, let the peace of God's presence seep through the racing thoughts of your mind and jumbled emotions in your chest; there is calm and clarity in his nearness. This is not out of reach; ask the Holy Spirit to impart God's tangible peace to you today.

Holy Spirit, I long to know your nearness today. Fill my mind and heart with the peace of your presence, the same peace that Jesus promised. I trust that you are better than I have known. Let your Word calm my anxious thoughts and your comfort bring peace to my aching heart. I am yours.

Present in Struggle

*Those who love me, I will deliver;
I will protect those who know my name.
When they call to me, I will answer them;
I will be with them in trouble,
I will rescue them and honor them.*

PSALM 91:14-15 NRSV

When we call on the Lord, he does not simply hear us. He works on our behalf and he answers us. He protects those who cry out to him for help. He rescues his beloved ones over and over again. He is present in the struggle, bringing comfort in the pain.

He is constant in companionship; he won't ever let us face any trial or trouble on our own. It doesn't matter how many times we fall into the same trap; he is always with us. Will we trust him to do what only he can do? He is faithful to his promises—every single one!

Constant One, never let me forget your consistent advocacy in my life. You are not simply fighting for me; you are with me in the trenches. Deliver me, God, and lift me out of the pit of my despair. Let me see once again that your hand of mercy is on my life.

Dare to Drink

Those who go to him for help are happy,
and they are never disgraced.

PSALM 34:5 NCV

When was the last time you came away from an encounter with the Lord filled with the satisfaction that you are deeply seen, known, and cared for by the King of kings? However long it has been, consider this your invitation for a fresh revelation of his compassion toward you today.

There is nothing like the love that your good and gracious Father bestows upon you. There is no hint of disappointment in his eyes, nor a tinge of regret hiding in his thoughts toward you. You are completely covered in the abundance of his pure affection. He delights in you. You are his pride and joy. Do not let your discouragement keep you from receiving his pure pleasure over you. Do you dare drink in his goodness today?

Loving Father, I approach your throne of mercy with an open heart, surrendered before you today. Let your thoughts toward me wash away the disappointment I feel in myself. I want to know the fullness of your love that revives my weary heart time and again. Do not hold back today; I am not holding back from you.

Gracious Guide

Now I can say to myself and to all,
"Relax and rest, be confident and serene,
for the Lord rewards fully those who simply trust in him."
PSALM 116:7 TPT

When we place our hands in the hand of Jesus, we will find that he is not an impatient leader. He is gentle and easy to please. He does not pull us along, dragging us behind him when we are unsure. He takes his time, patiently coaxing out our worries and hesitations. He is a partner and a gracious guide. His wisdom no one can outdo; with our lives joined to his, we will find that there is beauty in places we never knew to look.

In the trading of our heavy burdens, we are able to see what we could not focus on before. With Jesus as our teacher, we will learn to rest in the confidence of his ways. When we let him take the lead, he will refresh our souls along the way.

Jesus, you are the model of mercy and love that I want to follow. I give you my heavy burdens today and partner with you in life. I will follow your lead and trust your heart as you teach me to walk in your ways. I know that I can trust you.

No Empty Hope

This is no empty hope, for God himself is the one who has prepared us for this wonderful destiny. And to confirm this promise, he has given us the Holy Spirit, like an engagement ring, as a guarantee.

2 CORINTHIANS 5:5 TPT

Jesus' resurrection was just the beginning of the overwhelming victory we have access to in God's kingdom. We have fellowship with the Spirit of God who strengthens us when we are weak, empowers us to love when we have no cares left of our own, and who ministers to us through close companionship all the days of our lives.

We do not have to conjure anything up; no, the Spirit of God is living and active. May we awaken to the dynamic power of the Spirit that is already at work within our lives. His presence is the guarantee of his infinite goodness that is both here and to come.

Holy Spirit, I rely on your influence in my life in every area. I surrender to your power, and I ask for a deeper revelation of your goodness through the experience of your presence. I long for a glimpse of the glory to come.

Set Free

*"If you abide in My word, you are My disciples indeed.
And you shall know the truth, and the truth shall make you free."*

JOHN 8:31-32 NKJV

Where do you feel hemmed in today? Are there thought patterns that you can't escape? Is there worry that won't let up? Look into the Word of God and find higher perspective for your circumstances. His truth is lasting, and it will not fail you. The traps of the enemy will not keep you ensnared when you fix your mind on God's better ways.

Let the truth of God's magnanimous nature set you free today. You are free to live, to love, to try, and to fail. There is no experience that is left untouched by God's mercy. Will you take the risk of believing that God is as good as he says? You can place all your bets on him.

Living Love, I abide in your Word of truth that declares my freedom from fear and shame. I trust that you will never leave me, just as you have stated over and over again in your Word. As I align with the truth of your nature, I know that I will experience even more liberty.

Venture to Know

Those who know the Lord trust him,
because he will not leave those who come to him.
PSALM 9:10 NCV

How well do you know the Lord? Is your heart convinced of his goodness and mercy? Have you recognized the faithfulness of his hand of provision in your life? Whatever your response, know that there is always deeper fellowship to be found in him.

As you experience his consistent comfort in your life and his unmatched wisdom, you cannot help but grow to trust him more. He is a faithful Father and a loyal friend. He is a judicious counselor and a trustworthy advisor. He will never steer you wrong. Today, will you venture to know him more?

Lord, I can see your fingerprints on my life. I have known you in plenty and in want, but I have to know you more. I am not satisfied with yesterday's bread. Fill me with a fresh portion of your grace as I press into your presence.

Healing through Humility

Do not be wise in your own eyes;
fear the Lord and turn away from evil.
It will be healing to your body
and refreshment to your bones.

PROVERBS 3:7-8 NASB

When we turn toward the Lord in our hour of need, we can be sure that he will give us what we require. Let our hearts remain humble, trusting that God's ways are better than our own. We cannot dictate how life will go; there are myriads of elements out of our control. Only God sees how everything connects; he sees every detail. Pride clouds our vision and keeps us at an arm's length from help, but humility allows us to receive what we could never achieve on our own.

It is not foolishness to yield our hearts to the one who created them. In surrender, we find that it is his mercy that holds us up. There is healing when we rest in him; there is refreshing that comes when we lean back into the loving and capable arms of our good Father.

Lord my healer, I surrender my heart to yours again. I lean into your lavish love and trust that you will breathe your Spirit's life in me. Revive me in your living waters of mercy; I am yours.

Without a Veil

The world and its desires pass away,
but whoever does the will of God lives forever.

When the world feels overwhelming, where fears and uncertainties abound, there is a firm place for us to find our grounding. The ways and Word of God are everlasting; there is no end to his marvelous mercy. The world and its desires *will* pass away, but even when the breath leaves our bodies, we have not reached the end of our existence.

Though we taste the fruits of God's kingdom here and now, we have not yet seen the fullness of it. The worries of this life will be left behind, and we will live in the light of God's glorious love without even a veil to cloud our vision. In the meantime, there is so much goodness to discover. Follow the path of love, where your Savior leads you, and you will find it.

God, sometimes imagining the glory of your kingdom feels like wishful thinking. Then I look into your Word and find hints to even greater things than I could imagine. Lead me on in love as I walk with you through this life and into eternity.

Not a Moment

"Teach them to obey everything that I have taught you, and I will be with you always, even until the end of this age."

MATTHEW 28:20 NCV

In the struggle of not wanting to feel the depths of grief, yet being carried away by its tide, we can rest assured in this truth: God is with us. When the waves of sorrow sweep over us until we can feel nothing else, we are tethered to the anchor of God's love. He will not let us go.

There is not a moment where we drift from God's great grace. Not a single moment. When we are holding on for dear life, what we don't see is that we are held already in the grasp of his hand. Jesus himself said it: "I will be with you always." If we have not reached the end, we can be sure that he has not left us.

My God, I admit that there have been moments in my grief when I questioned where you were. Even when I thought you had abandoned me, you were closer than my breath. When I cry myself to sleep, you are singing songs of healing over my broken heart. Let me sense your nearness now.

Stay Closer

Even if my father and mother abandon me,
the Lord will hold me close.
PSALM 27:10 NLT

There is one who stays closer to us than our family. Even if our dearest friends and blood relatives were to turn away and leave us, the Lord would draw us closer to himself. He never abandons us, not even when we run into a den of thieves that he warns us about. There he is, running right with us, ready to deliver us from our own foolishness.

If this is what God is like, why do we worry? We are never alone, and there is no shadow of shame that could keep the light of his love from shining on us. He is better than the purest love we've ever known. He is more purposeful than the best intentions of any other. In everything, he is there with all the strength of his mercy and the compassion of his heart.

Lord, you have been so good to me. You are more loyal than my closest confidants, and I know that I will continue to taste the goodness of your faithfulness in my life. Hold me close today in your mercy.

Armor of Loyalty

It is impossible for God to lie for we know that his promise and his vow will never change! And now we have run into his heart to hide ourselves in his faithfulness. This is where we find his strength and comfort, for he empowers us to seize what has already been established ahead of time—an unshakeable hope.

HEBREWS 6:18 TPT

Let today be the day you run into God's heart. Hide yourself in his faithfulness; his loyalty is armor around you. Let the peace of his constant presence guard your heart and mind. There is comfort for your sorrow and consolation for your disappointed hopes. Everything you long for can be found in him.

Place the love of God like a seal upon your heart, that you may remember his constancy every time you need the reminder. There is no better time to surrender yourself to the great embrace of your loving Father. As he speaks his Words of life over you, you will find that your heart blooms in love's light.

Good Father, I run into your heart of love today. I know it's big enough to hold me as well as every other who comes to you. Will you love me to life in your presence again? I long for the strength and comfort that comes from resting in you. Do it again, Lord; fill me with hope.

North Star

All flesh is like grass and all its glory like the flower of grass.
The grass withers, and the flower falls,
but the word of the Lord remains forever.

1 PETER 1:24-25 ESV

In a world where transitions and change are inevitable, it can be hard to gain your bearings when looking outside of yourself. Seasons change, and with it, flowers bloom and fade. Grass grows and it withers. Life is birthed in some, while death takes others away.

But there is an anchor for the soul that cannot be moved. The Word of the Lord is his covenant and it is the plumb line we can align our lives to. The same Creator God who breathed life into dry bones and made them live is the God who calls us his own. His intentions have not wavered from the affection he started out with. May we always look to him as our north star, our guiding light.

Faithful One, though my heart is battered by the storm of loss, you have not left me. I set my eyes on you, Constant One. You are loyal in love as ever you have been. I trust you with my life; encourage my heart in your consistent goodness again today.

No Expiration Date

The Lord God helps me,
Therefore, I am not disgraced;
Therefore, I have set my face like flint,
And I know that I will not be ashamed.
ISAIAH 50:7 NASB

When we build our lives upon the firm foundation of God's faithfulness, no quakes of the earth or gale-force storms can move us from his help. He will not let us be destroyed by the winds of adversity, and we won't be swept away by the chaotic tide of the world and its wearying ways.

Let this be our confidence: God is our very present help. There is no expiration date on his support. He is always with us, working for our good. When we are exhausted by the worries of this life, there is an invitation to a greater perspective. Let us peel off the apprehensions of our hearts and watch God work on our behalf.

God my help, I remember today that you are with me and you never change. You help me over and over again, and somehow you never tire of doing it. I release my concerns to you and let the confidence of your continued support be the thing I set my mind upon.

Overflowing Fountain

Fill us with your love every morning.
Then we will sing and rejoice all our lives.
PSALM 90:14 NCV

Are you empty of hope today? Are you running low on strength? There is an overflowing fountain of love to fill you up. Every morning is a new opportunity to receive God's mercy in unending measure. Every moment is an invitation for you to be washed in the waterfall of God's affection.

God's love never fails, and it won't stop now. Let it be your courage, your strength, and your song. The flow of its tide never recedes; it is always rising over you. God's pure pleasure is its source, and it never runs dry. Let your mind be washed in its waves. Let your heart be cleansed by its living waters. Nothing in your life is left untouched. You are covered.

Lord, your love is the song that lifts hope to my lips. I have tasted before, but I long for more. Let me be refreshed and satisfied in the pure springs of your kindness today. I welcome you to wash over me.

Simple Requirements

The teaching of your word gives light,
so even the simple can understand.
PSALM 119:130 NLT

God's wisdom does not need a translator. With his Spirit as your teacher and his Word as your guidebook, you will find that the light of revelation shines in simple clarity. Often, his wisdom seems too simple to be true. God's Word says that he chose things the world considers foolish in order to shame those who think they are wise (1 Corinthians 1:27). Simply put, those who think they know better often dismiss the value of simple truth.

Complex thought does not equal wisdom. Look through the Word of God and you will find that his requirements are simple, though they are not easy. Love sounds like a worthy pursuit until your preferences are tested. Follow God's ways, and do not overcomplicate them. You will find life in your pursuit of loyal love.

Wise God, I submit myself to your way. I'm done trying to figure out complex theological thought and break it down. You have already done the breaking down: I will follow your law of love through the hills and valleys of this life.

Dive Headfirst

*The Lord is faithful, who will establish you
and guard you from the evil one.*

2 THESSALONIANS 3:3 NKJV

In the throes of grief, it can feel like everything has been thrown into question. But even in the questioning, there is a bedrock of loyal love that holds us up. It can hold the weight of our sorrow and our doubts. We often take what we have for granted until loss, or the threat of it, sends us reeling.

You don't have to have it all together to know that God's faithfulness is still your portion. He cannot be talked out of his loyalty, and he cannot be convinced to leave you. Let him into this process—even the questioning. He is with you through it all. He welcomes your overwhelming emotions with open arms. Do not hold back for his sake; dive headfirst into all of it, knowing he will not let you be lost. What you're looking for will be found in the wrestling.

God, I trust that you can handle me as I am today. I don't even know how to express what I feel, the utter heartbreak that has ripped me open. But I trust that as I wade through it all with you, you will make wrong things right and heal my gaping wounds.

Not a Beggar

*"Let anyone who is thirsty
come to me and drink."*
JOHN 7:37 NIV

In the intensity of your deep need, God meets you with his mercy. Look to him today and you will see that he has more than enough to satisfy your greatest cravings. You are not a beggar in the kingdom of God. There is abundance in his house, and you are his beloved child!

What do you need today? God has not forgotten you, and he is not ignorant of the trials you face. Simply open your hands to receive what God is willingly pouring over you. There is more beauty than you can imagine in his goodness. Take heart; he is here for you with the help you need.

Lord, I can't pretend that sometimes the depth of my need doesn't overwhelm my trust in you. When I remember who you are and what you've already done, how could I not open up to you again? You are faithful. Draw near to me with the promise of your love and cause my heart to hope again as you provide for me.

Where Hope Grows

In hope we have been saved,
but hope that is seen is not hope;
for who hopes for what he already sees.
ROMANS 8:24 NASB

As long as you draw breath into your lungs and your heart pumps blood through your chest, you have not reached the end of hope. It is the string that connects us to the coming kingdom of our God. What you see as lack in your life is an opportunity to grab hold of hope in that area. It is not vain because it is completely dependent on God's unchanging promises, not on what you can make happen on your own.

Let hope rise again as you look at your current circumstances as an invitation for God's great provision. Remind yourself of the promises of his Word and let them fill the space where hope grows. Let the time of waiting be a place of sowing seeds of expectation in God's faithful goodness.

Holy One, you are perfect in lovingkindness that doesn't miss a detail. I trust you to continue to lead me in love all the days of my life. Feed my weak hope with the sustenance of your strong mercy, and it will grow. I believe that you are good and that you are for me.

No Doubt

"The Spirit of the LORD is upon me, and he has anointed me to be hope for the poor, freedom for the brokenhearted, and new eyes for the blind, and to preach to prisoners, 'You are set free!' I have come to share the message of Jubilee, for the time of God's great acceptance has begun."
LUKE 4:18-19 TPT

When we are poor in spirit, we are given a hope that is greater than our circumstances. When we are brokenhearted, God leads us into greater freedom as he expands our ability to experience his love in the healing of our deep pain. When we are confined by fear, shame, or doubt, he has already set us free from the weight of it; he has taken our heavy load and he gives us the light load of his peace.

We belong to the family of God. He is the King of kings and the Lord of lords. He is the creator and the sustainer. He is love. We belong to love. Why would we disqualify ourselves from his acceptance when he has done all the work of ushering us into his great mercy?

Spirit of God, fill me today with the hope of my calling. Lead me into greater freedom as I walk in your ways. Let every doubt of worthiness float away in the flood of your abundant love pouring over me. You are so, so good, and I belong to you.

Stronger in Hope

"Let us praise the Lord, the God of Israel,
because he has come to help his people
and has given them freedom.
He has given us a powerful Savior."
LUKE 1:68-69 NCV

It doesn't matter how dire your circumstances are: God is more powerful. He is mighty to save, and he will not let you go. Today, let the praise of God be on your lips as you remember how he has shown up for those he loves over and over again. He has never failed, and he won't stop now.

His faithfulness is your shield; it will cover you from the fiery darts of the enemy. His power is great, and it is working on your behalf. He is working on your behalf. Let the weight of worry lift as you raise your awareness to God's greatness again today. Don't be silent, for in your confession, your heart will grow stronger in hope.

Powerful One, you are brighter than the morning sun and more constant than the moon's glow at night. As I look to you today, I remember your greatness. You are better than I give you credit for, and for that, I am both eternally grateful and hopeful. I wait on your next move.

Most Trustworthy

The LORD is for me; he will help me.
I will look in triumph at those who hate me.
It is better to take refuge in the LORD
than to trust in people.
PSALM 118:7-8 NLT

When you consider the most trustworthy people in your life, who comes to mind? How do they show up for you? Even the most faithful friend will disappoint your expectations at some point. But there is one who does not forget a single promise he has made. He does not get distracted, though his timing is not your own.

Lay all your trust on God today. He will help you, no stipulations about it. He will lead you in his mercy and surround you with his peace. Even when your friends fail you, he won't. He is a safe place to rest in the security of trust. He is faithful, beloved, and he will never leave you.

Worthy God, I put my trust in you again today. I have no other place to turn, and I know that I don't need any alternatives. Cover me in the blanket of your presence and awaken my heart to life again.

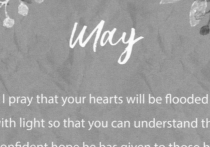

May

I pray that your hearts will be flooded
with light so that you can understand the
confident hope he has given to those he
called—his holy people who are his rich
and glorious inheritance.

EPHESIANS 1:18 NLT

Garden of Growth

O Lord; give ear to my pleas for mercy!
In your faithfulness answer me, in your righteousness!
PSALM 143:1 ESV

When all hope feels lost and you cannot see what once seemed clear for the fog of grief that surrounds you, let your honest cry for help ring out. God has not left you, no matter how lonely your sorrow feels. He is the God who sits with us in our devastation, comforting us. But he does not stop there; he is our redeemer, turning even our darkest moments into a garden of growth and glory.

Cry out to your good shepherd today if you struggle to sense his presence. He is closer than you know. He will never ignore your pleas for mercy, so don't hold back. He is not disappointed in the state of your heart; be honest with him and with yourself. As you recognize where you're at, you can more clearly see the mercy of God meeting you in the middle.

Spirit of God, I cry out to you from the depths of my heart today. I won't pretend to have it all together or to be in a surer place of faith than I feel at the moment. Meet me in my desperation and my loss. Touch the deepest parts of my pain with your healing presence.

Comforting Words

The precepts of the LORD are right,
giving joy to the heart.
The commands of the LORD are radiant,
giving light to the eyes.

PSALM 19:8 NIV

There is comfort to be found in the truth of God's Word and consolation in his wisdom. He knows just what we need right when we need it. If we are feeling a little lost in the weeds of our sorrow, and it is hard to remember God's promises, let us look into his Word for clarity.

His wisdom is not for the elite; it is not reserved for some and withheld from others who are seeking. It is his heart laid out for all in the same measure. There is joy to be found in the revelation of his wonderful nature. When God instructs, he does so with love as his motivation. He reveals his compassion through his teachings over and over again. Come and fill up today on the Word of God that brings life.

Lord, only you know exactly what I need in this moment. Lead me in love as I read and meditate on your Word. Speak clearly to me today and bring comfort to my weary heart.

Steady Hand

You in Your mercy have led forth the people whom You have redeemed;
You have guided them in Your strength to Your holy habitation.
EXODUS 15:13 NKJV

God's mercy is never dependent upon us. It is the outflow of his very nature; his love propels him to lead us into redemption and healing. We have been called by God, and we are his children. May our hearts find rest in the confidence and competence of God's steady hand of mercy leading our lives.

It is not our weakness that defines us; it is God's strength that determines our outcome. May today be the day we find certainty, not in what we can do but in what God will do for us. He is full of kindness, leading us into freedom continually until we stand face-to-face with him.

Merciful One, I give up the impossible standards I have set for myself; I only keep disappointing myself over and over again. I know that you don't require perfection—far from it. You will lead me into your strength no matter how little I have of my own. Empower me as I surrender to you once again.

Feet of Jesus

Come, let us bow down in worship,
let us kneel before the LORD our Maker.
PSALM 95:6 NIV

Today, lay down every overwhelming thought and feeling at the feet of Jesus. Even if just for a few moments, let your attention focus on him. As you bow before him, letting the weight of his goodness replace the weight of your worries, let his love wash over you.

The demands of the day dim in the present nearness of embodied love. Let his presence be the oil that seeps into your mind, quieting the chaos of racing thoughts. Let his words sink deep into the soil of your heart, sowing life into the deepest parts of you. Let him be the vision you seek. He is infinitely better than your wildest dreams suggest.

Savior, I kneel before you today, letting my focus drift from my current sadness to your timeless goodness. You are the hope of my life, and I long for a fresh touch of your mercy. As I look to you, give me vision to see you looking back at me.

Expanded Understanding

*Wise people can also listen and learn;
even they can find good advice in these words.*

PROVERBS 1:5 NCV

Every day is a new opportunity to revel in the wisdom of our great God and King. There is always more to learn: more revelation of his love, more solutions to problems, more knowledge of the ways of God's kingdom. As long as we are drawing breath in our lungs, there is more to receive.

Will we see the opportunity in our present circumstances to learn more of God's ways? Even through pain, sorrow, and hardship there is a multitude of lessons we can learn about God's nature. Our pain is not our punishment; it does, however, teach us and expand our understanding if we let it.

Wise God, I know that you work all things together for my good. Even in my greatest suffering, you increase my capacity to receive your love and provision. I depend on you, giver of good gifts. Will you show me the treasures that are being birthed in the midst of the darkness of this season?

A Foretaste

All praise to God, the Father of our Lord Jesus Christ.
It is by his great mercy that we have been born again,
because God raised Jesus Christ from the dead.
Now we live with great expectation.
1 PETER 1:3 NLT

In the resurrection power of Jesus, we are brought to life again. We have hope for the future—bright shining hope. It is with great expectation that we look ahead to the day of the return of our Savior. He will usher in the age of his kingdom, once for all. There will be no more suffering, no more fear, and no more shame.

The obstacles that seem insurmountable now will look like anthills when we view them from the perspective of eternity. Even today there is the invitation to look from heaven's view over our lives. May we courageously lay hold of the promise of complete restoration and lift our gaze to the restorer of all things.

Glorious Lord, there is so much to look forward to when I look with expectant eyes toward the fulfillment of your promises. You reveal yourself through the tangible mercy of your miracles working out in my life. But it is all but a foretaste of what is to come. Let my heart hold to the hope of your coming goodness.

Turned Over

*"Don't worry. For your Father cares deeply
about even the smallest detail of your life."*
MATTHEW 10:30-31 TPT

The worries of life do not stop knocking on the doors of our hearts. We don't have to go looking for them, for the unknown meets us every day. How we respond to them is up to us. Will we feed on the fear of what-ifs and how-comes? Or will we submit them to the truth of God's consistent nature?

Even if we forget how good our Father is, he will not change his ways. He is the same yesterday, today, and forever. His truth stands firm, whether or not we recognize it. Surrender is a practice. There is no pressure to get it right every time; God is not looking for perfection. Our awareness is the key to our submission. We can turn our worries over to our Good Father whenever we realize that we are holding onto them.

Father, I will not waste regret on yesterday or spend too much time wondering about how I will respond in the future. Right here and now, I submit my thoughts to you. I give you the weight of my worries, taking instead the covering of your constant compassion. Renew me as I rest in your confidence.

Ever-flowing Tide

Do not, O LORD, withhold your mercy from me;
let your steadfast love and your faithfulness
keep me safe forever.
PSALM 40:11 NRSV

God's mercy is an ever-flowing tide that covers everything in its path. There you are, wading in its depths already. Lay back and let yourself drift in its vastness. Let its waves wash over you, and you will be refreshed in the cleansing waters. God does not withhold even a drop of lovingkindness from you today.

No state of mind disqualifies you from God's grace. It does not matter what you've done or not done, what you've believed or not believed. God's grace is yours all the same. Drink deeply of his goodness; you are worthy because he has said you are. Don't close yourself off to what he freely offers you today. Open up and let his mercy flood you.

Merciful God, your kindness seems too great a gift for me to receive so freely. But oh, how I long for it! I lay aside my doubt and my feelings of unworthiness and invite you in. I want your mercy more than I can say; I need it. Wash over me with the rushing tide of your love, and I will be revived.

Carried by Grace

In all their affliction He was afflicted,
And the angel of His presence saved them;
In His love and in His mercy He redeemed them,
And He lifted them and carried them all the days of old.

ISAIAH 63:9 NASB

The God who led his people out of the wilderness into their Promised Land is the same God who leads us out of our captivity into the great expanse of his liberty. He carries us when we cannot put one foot in front of the other; in his love and mercy he holds us.

Jesus knew the pain of sorrow, and he carried the weight of suffering when he walked this earth. In his dying, love itself was laid down once and for all, and in his resurrection, death was brought to its knees. There is no pain we experience that Jesus has not already gone through. We can rest in the support of his mercy that upholds us.

Redeemer, thank you for bearing my pain. Ease the heaviness of it today as I rest in your capable arms. Carry me through this storm, for I cannot see the ground beneath my feet.

Redemptive Power

LORD, you are my God;
I will exalt you and praise your name,
for in perfect faithfulness you have done wonderful things,
things planned long ago.

ISAIAH 25:1 NIV

The ways of God are a marvelous mystery to our finite understanding. And yet, our comprehension grows as we watch him work out his promises in faithful love. He is worthy of our admiration, for what he does is wonderful. He takes the weakest things of this world and imbues them with his strength. He gives beauty to the ashes of defeat and his joy dawns brightly after the darkest night.

He is not finished with us yet. There are promises yet to be fulfilled. He sees it all so clearly; we can trust his methods and his timing. He is wiser than we could ever imagine. He has a plan for us, and he won't let a single thing go to waste in our lives. Even our greatest suffering will reveal the greatness of his redemptive power. Take hope.

Mighty God, you are the one I bet my life on. I trust that you are not done working your miraculous wonders in my life. What looks like utter destruction to me is a field of opportunity for your loyal love to sow seeds of restoration. Give me eyes to see you.

Declared Innocent

The Lord God is like a sun and shield;
the Lord gives us kindness and honor.
He does not hold back anything good
from those whose lives are innocent.

PSALM 84:11 NCV

When you read the above Scripture, how does it make you feel? Does it bring you comfort to know that God offers you kindness and honor? Or did your heart sink a little when you read that God does not hold back from those whose lives are innocent? If you were quick to disqualify yourself, let your heart and mind find rest in this: you are wrapped up in Jesus Christ, and he has declared your innocence.

If you are still struggling with doubt, lay it before God. Invite him to speak his truth over your mind even now, bringing wisdom and understanding. You are wholly accepted by God, and you are firmly rooted in his kingdom. He will not hold back anything good from you, for you are his and he is your good and faithful Father.

Kind Father, I long to know the truth of who I am in you. I don't want to be swayed by doubt or fear of not being or doing enough. I know that your mercy does not require my perfection, but I still struggle to know my own innocence. Fill me with your presence and break down the lies of shame that have kept me from seeing what you see when you look at me.

Peace in Turbulence

He awoke and rebuked the wind and said to the sea, "Peace! Be still!"
And the wind ceased, and there was a great calm.

MARK 4:39 ESV

The same Jesus who spoke to the stormy seas and calmed them is the one who speaks peace over your turbulence. He brings the chaos to rest with just a word. What's even more, is you have the Spirit of the living God inside of you. You have authority to calm the tumultuous winds that threaten your life.

Where there is anxiety, speak peace over it. Where there is overwhelming worry, command the thoughts to be still. See what this does for your well-being. Everything that Jesus did when he walked this earth, he instructed that we would do—and even more! Let your confidence rise as you practice in faith what Jesus taught.

Peace Bringer, even when I don't know what to do, you are my strong and mighty tower. You speak to the wind and the waves and they obey your voice! I know that you will do the same for me when I don't know how to help myself. Teach me to walk in your ways and live with confidence in your mighty Word.

Essence of Truth

The very essence of your words is truth;
all your just regulations will stand forever.
PSALM 119:160 NLT

Not a word departs from the mouth of God that does not find its purpose and fulfillment. What he says goes. What he promised, he will surely provide. May our hearts be rooted in the immoveable foundation of God's faithfulness.

Though we make many plans for our lives, not all will manifest. But what God says is his vow. He leads us always in loyal love, and he never goes back on his Word. Though our own consistency waxes and wanes, his never wavers. Will we take him at his Word, or do we project our own failures and shortcomings onto him? Let today be the day we decide to rest in the confidence of his constant nature.

Everlasting Lord, who else is there like you in all the earth? You never lie or mislead us with empty promises. You always come through every single time. May I adjust my lens of life so I see through your broad perspective that takes the bigger picture into account. You are faithful and you always will be.

Sweet Message

*The Messiah has come to preach this sweet message of peace to you,
the ones who were distant, and to those who are near.*
EPHESIANS 2:17 TPT

No matter what life throws our way, we are found in the all-encompassing mercy of our great God and King. There is not a circumstance or a trial that can cause God to lift his love from our lives. In every turn of the road, there is love incarnate with peace as his offering.

God is not more faithful to us in our joys and celebrations than he is in our devastation and our sorrows. He is the same. He is good, and he will never change. May we drink deeply of his goodness today as we meditate on the sweetness of his perfect peace that is ours in Christ.

Messiah, you are the fulfillment of the promised peace of God. You are the one I lean into today; may it be true of my every moment. I want to experience the tangible goodness of your presence with me. Fill me up again!

Secret Strength

I know what it is to be in need, and I know what it is to have plenty.
I have learned the secret of being content in any and every situation,
whether well fed or hungry, whether living in plenty or in want.
I can do all this through him who gives me strength.

PHILIPPIANS 4:12-13 NIV

Have you learned the secret that Paul lived his life by? There is no season of plenty or of lack that can dictate the unrelenting love of God that is always flowing in abundance over you. When you learn to find your contentment in what is available to you in the present moment, then you find the strength to fuel you for anything you face. When you receive God's love, you have love to give.

Let God's grace be the sustenance that empowers you. There is nothing you have need of that he does not provide. You can do all things, walk through all kinds of situations, and press on in love when you rely on the support of the God who walks with you hand in hand. Whatever you are facing today, you have the source of life as your strong support and deep well of wisdom.

Holy Spirit, I know that you are with me. I ask for greater awareness when you strengthen me to do what I cannot accomplish on my own. You are everything I need; give me the same power that Paul experienced that I may always sing your praises.

Fruit of Satisfaction

The kingdom of God is not eating and drinking,
but righteousness and peace and joy in the Holy Spirit.
ROMANS 14:17 NASB

There is so much available to us in the Spirit. There is the sunshine of God's peace, the river of his joy, and the fruit of his righteousness. There is an abundance that far exceeds what can be consumed. There is no lack that we experience that cannot be completely overwhelmed by the generosity of his kingdom.

Every area of your life is already covered by the kindness of your faithful Father. He will not let you go hungry, and he won't leave you dying of thirst. This is just the bare minimum; God is clear that he will always provide for your needs. What is it that you long for beyond the necessary? Seek his fulfillment, and you will not be sorry you did.

Holy Spirit, fill me with the fruit of your presence in my life. I don't want to be surprised every time you satisfy a need; I want to hope for so much more and expect it with the confidence of a well-loved child. Satisfy what I don't even know to ask for—the longings deep within.

Purity of Kindness

The LORD is righteous in everything he does;
he is filled with kindness.

PSALM 145:17 NLT

When you think about God the Father, what traits come to mind? Do you know him as a kind and gracious Father, or do you think of him as apathetic? Perhaps you think that his pleasure in you is dependent on your performance. God is a better Father than our earthly dads. He is perfect in his intentions toward us, never clouded by misgivings, for he sees us clearly. His love is full and unrelenting.

Everything God does, he does in mercy. His justice is firm, and his virtue is unmoving. He is full of kindness today and always. Take time to fellowship with your generous Father today and find your heart filled with his delight over you!

Righteous One, you are unmatched in your love. I cannot even imagine the purity of your kindness. I want to receive your affection without my own thoughts of worthiness getting in the way. You are my good Father, and I trust that your mercy's power is not exaggerated.

Look No Further

Since we have been justified by faith,
we have peace with God through our Lord Jesus Christ.
ROMANS 5:1 ESV

Peace with God is not some elite, unattainable reward. It is the gift of God through Jesus. It is yours today and every day. You have communion with the Spirit of the living God, given through Christ. There is nothing more for you to do or be in order to receive his perfect peace.

Come as you are today to the banqueting table of God's love. He has reserved a place for you, and it will never be filled by another. Enter into the peace of his presence where he offers all that you need. He has all that you have been looking for. Stop your searching; here is the fulfillment you long for, right here and now, in his presence.

Jesus, I am so thankful that you already paved the way to unhindered fellowship with the Father. Lead me, Spirit, into the courts of my King where I will find all that I have longed for. Your peace is my plentiful portion today.

Hallmark of Friendship

You, Sovereign LORD,
help me for your name's sake;
out of the goodness of your love, deliver me.
PSALM 109:21 NIV

In a world of shifting expectations, where change is inevitable and constancy in comfort is sought after, there are only a handful of things that remain consistent. God, never changing in love, is a firm foundation of steadiness. Though he has not changed, he is so much bigger and better than we can hold in our understanding in any given moment. The more we get to know him, the expansion of his goodness in our comprehension grows deeper.

God's mercy and kindness are the hallmark of his friendship. As a friend of God, you are the recipient of his generous love. Open up to the depth of his goodness and marvel in the revelations of his enormity today.

Lord, I long for a fresh glimpse of your incomparable goodness. Fill me with your wisdom that I may taste and eat of the fruit of your Spirit's life in mine. Answer me today as I turn to you.

Covered by Covenant

I know that you will welcome me into your house,
for I am covered by your covenant of mercy and love.
So I come to your sanctuary with deepest awe
to bow in worship and adore you.

PSALM 5:7 TPT

The promises of God are a covering over your life. They are the banner of God's unrelenting love for you. You are part of a large family of beloved children of the Father of lights. He has spoken freedom and peace over his beloved ones and given his Spirit as a seal of his covenant.

As you connect with him today, let awe lead you. Let the wonder of being called his own guide you. Fellowship as children do with their parents; share all that you have been holding with him, and watch his response. Listen for his words of wisdom and eat them up. Delight today in the union of your heart and his.

Merciful Father, thank you for removing every hindrance that kept me from knowing you in clarity and truth. As I connect with you through your Spirit, fill me with your wisdom. I will not hold back my love from you, and I know you never do!

Running In

How priceless is your unfailing love, O God!
People take refuge in the shadow of your wings.
They feast on the abundance of your house;
you give them drink from your river of delights.
For with you is the fountain of life;
in your light we see light.

PSALM 36:7-9 NIV

The presence of God is full of abundant life. He meets us wherever we find ourselves in the moment, and he offers us the refreshing waters of his goodness. His love is like a treasure-trove; it is impossible to measure its wealth. We have full access to the storehouses of his mercy. What a wonderful Father!

In the light of God's presence, we see what once remained hidden. As we seek his wisdom, the eyes of our hearts are enlightened by his truth. There is so much more beauty than we can imagine hidden just within the realm of his fellowship. May we enter in with expectancy, no more hanging around the open door of his generous heart. It's time to dive in.

God, you are so lavish in your love. I know that I could live off what flows from you into my life without ever pressing in for more. But why would I settle for that when I have access to so much more? Today, I'm done passively receiving from you. I'm running right into your heart!

Active Promises

They shall neither hunger nor thirst,
Neither heat nor sun shall strike them;
For He who has mercy on them will lead them,
Even by the springs of water He will guide them.

ISAIAH 49:10 NKJV

If you are feeling the pressure of your circumstances today, know that this is not the end. It will not break you. The Lord your God has mercy on you, and he has promised to lead you. He will refresh your soul with the living water of his presence. His active promises are working in your life even now.

Follow your shepherd today and lean into his voice. He will give you what you need. He will fulfill the longings of your heart with the abundance of his love. There is no need to fear the unknown, for God sees everything clearly and he will not lead you to a place he himself would not go. To the ends of the earth, he is with you.

Shepherd of my soul, I'm following where you lead me. I know that you have not left me to figure anything out on my own. May my life be hidden in the covering of your merciful kindness until I stand face-to-face with you in glory. I trust you.

The Final Word

He saved us, not on the basis of deeds which we have done in righteousness, but according to His mercy, by the washing of regeneration and renewing by the Holy Spirit.

TITUS 3:5 NASB

What a relief it is to know that our salvation is not dependent on us but on the mercy of God. Though we are limited in generosity of heart, our Father is inexhaustible in his love. He does not withhold from us even an ounce of his affectionate kindness.

We have been rescued from the clutches of death and have been given the hope of eternal, abundant life in God's kingdom. The grave does not have the final word. The resurrected Christ does. His love pours over and into our lives from the wealth of his heart through his Spirit. We are revived and renewed in his presence.

Holy One, you are the life source that sustains every breath. Refresh me in the living waters of your presence again. Oh, how I long for my heart to come alive in you once more.

None More Loyal

The Lord keeps you from all harm and watches over your life.
The Lord keeps watch over you as you come and go,
both now and forever.

PSALM 121:7-8 NLT

Do you feel alone in your experience? Is there solitude in your sorrow? Turn your attention to the living God again today. He is closer than you know. His gaze has not left you for a moment, and he is not oblivious to any need you have yet to name.

He cares for you in loyalty and with honor. He does not force your face to look at him. He is gentle, and he is faithful whether or not you're watching him. Rest in the knowledge of your good God fighting on your behalf today. He is your advocate and your defender. He will always lead you in love no matter how you follow.

Loving Lord, your character is incomprehensible. I have never known a more loyal lover. My own parents weren't as attentive and caring as you are. You are the best thing in my life. May I have eyes to see what you are doing and may my heart be quick to recognize your voice.

Look Differently

To you I lift up my eyes,
O you who are enthroned in the heavens!
PSALM 123:1 NRSV

Where have your eyes been focused lately? Have they been downcast with the heaviness of your sorrow? Have they been fixated on the problems that have yet to be solved in your life? Wherever your focus has been, there is an invitation to look differently today.

The God of all the universe is constantly caring for you. All power and dominion are his, and he never fails. Will you lift your eyes to him today? Will you turn your attention to the one who is captured by yours? He is full of kindness and compassion. Look up and find him. He has not left you.

Great God, I can get so caught up in the demands of today that I forget to look at you. I don't want to waste my life overly focused on what doesn't matter. As I lift my eyes to you, will you give me the perspective of your great love over my life?

Refocus

We don't focus our attention on what is seen but on what is unseen.
For what is seen is temporary, but the unseen realm is eternal.

2 CORINTHIANS 4:18 TPT

When we are overwhelmed by the intensity of our current circumstances, it can be a difficult task to see anything beyond them. The Lord is gracious with us in every situation, and he does not degrade us when we have trouble focusing on him.

The turning of our attention is a practice, not something to be achieved once and made perfect. As we graciously practice refocusing our lens on Christ, we will learn to recognize the hope of glory in our midst. Let us keep redirecting our gaze to the eternal God whenever we think of it. We will not be disappointed when we do.

Christ Jesus, hope of glory, I direct my attention to you here and now. I remember your goodness as I look past the temporary pain of my present circumstances. I rely on your love to get me through. Give me your perspective so I can hope again.

Finishing Last

I have fought the good fight,
I have finished the race,
I have kept the faith.
2 TIMOTHY 4:7 NCV

In the race of life, it is not finishing first that matters. In fact, it could be said that finishing last would be preferable. What is important is that we run with endurance, knowing that what lies ahead of us will be worth us pressing on. May we remember that we have everything we need to finish well through the Holy Spirit who guides, encourages, and teaches us along the way.

We have every provision we need for every leg of life right when we need it. There is not a shortage of supplies; we have only to receive the grace offered to us in every moment. Let's keep going, eyes fixed on what lies ahead. And when fog rolls in and we have trouble seeing, let's follow the voice that directs us still.

Great God, lead me on in this race called life that I may not give up in my weariness. Support me with your strong arm so I can keep going. I rely on you, and I trust that you will keep me close as we continue this journey together.

Choose Forgiveness

*Be kind to each other, tenderhearted, forgiving one another,
just as God through Christ has forgiven you.*

EPHESIANS 4:32 NLT

In the light of the kindness we receive, we are able to give it with equal measure. We have received immeasurable compassion from our great God. Can we also not offer compassion to those in our lives? It is not weak to forgive those who offend or wrong us. It is strength to imitate God's mercy.

When faced with the opportunity to either extend or withhold grace, may we choose to align ourselves in God's extravagant love. As those who have been on the receiving end of God's kindness, may we remember the humility of our humanity. There is nothing greater than laying down our own pride in favor of love.

Merciful Father, I want to be like you in compassionate mercy. When I am tempted to let offense take root in my heart, would you lead me back to the truth of your love? I don't want to keep a running record of wrongs with those I love when you don't do that with me.

The Better Way

The word of the Lord is upright,
and all his work is done in faithfulness.
PSALM 33:4 ESV

There is no better way to be found in all the earth than the way of love. The Word of the Lord stands firm forever, and it's always being worked out in the faithfulness of God's unchanging character. Let us give up our search for the quick fixes of life and lean into the process that makes us pure in his image.

When we avoid the painful things in life or the hard work of building honest connection with ourselves and others, we prolong the process of our healing. There is no bypass for lasting change; it requires consistency and compassion. When we allow what we go through to grow our understanding of life, love, and the one who holds it all together, we walk in the way of transformative mercy.

Lord, you are faithful in all your ways. You don't throw a Band-Aid on a protruding bone and call it healed. You are the one who sets it right in its place. May I follow you in truth and venture into the unknown places without trying to speed past them. I want to know you in the grand experiences of life and in the minute details.

Process Invitation

*Do you despise the riches of His goodness, forbearance,
and longsuffering, not knowing that the goodness of God
leads you to repentance?*

ROMANS 2:4 NKJV

Are you sick and tired of hearing how good God is? If so, look deeper. What comes up for you? There's no use in ignoring where you're at or pretending to be in a better place. Get real today with your heart. How does it respond to the idea of God's goodness?

There is no shame in your current state. If you are struggling with believing that he is good, or even feeling anger toward him, this is a sign of something within you that needs to be met with his love. Will you invite him into your process right now? Only he knows exactly what you need, and he is the best counselor. Let him meet you in the middle of your mess. He is willing and able.

God, I want to know your goodness—to really know it. But I need you to meet me where I'm at today, where I'm struggling to see it at all in my life. Holy Spirit, I invite you into my questions, into my doubts, and into the offense in my heart. Speak to me with your words of life.

No Bias

"I will have mercy on whom I have mercy,
and I will have compassion on whom I have compassion."
ROMANS 9:15 NRSV

It is not our duty in life to manage the reactions and emotions of others. We can only truly change our own outlook on life not control others' viewpoints. We are responsible ultimately to ourselves and to God. That is not to say that we do not love others and treat them with respect, compassion, and kindness. Surely, that is the way of the cross.

May everything we do be saturated with the mercy that God bestows upon us. There is none who deserves it more than another. God is not biased in his views of humanity, except in extravagant love. Let us look through the lens of his compassion today and catch a glimpse of his perspective. As we receive more of his mercy that meets us where we are, we will be ready to extend the same to others.

Compassionate One, you are so full of love to all who call on you. May I never forget the depths of your mercy. As I receive, may I also pour out on others without a need for anything in return. I want to see both others and myself the way you do. Give me eyes to see!

June

"Whatever you ask in prayer, believe that
you have received it, and it will be yours."

MARK 11:24 ESV

Unbroken Vow

Be strong and courageous.
Do not be afraid or terrified because of them,
for the LORD your God goes with you;
he will never leave you nor forsake you.

DEUTERONOMY 31:6 NIV

Strength of spirit does not come from our own abilities. It relies on the support and power of our great God who is with us. Courage is not found in empty promises of vague goodness; it is in the confidence of the powerful love of our Savior that works in our lives. It is greater than our biggest fears.

Fear shouts at us with warnings of what could be, when faith fills us with the assurance that it doesn't matter what comes because God is by our side. He will never leave us; he will never abandon us. That is his promise, and his vow is an unbroken agreement to his people. He is with us. He is *always* with us.

Gracious God, let the truth of your nearness grow in my heart with confidence. You give me the courage to do what you lead me to with the strength of your presence. With you by my side, I lack nothing.

Strength to Live

God, being rich in mercy, because of His great love with which He loved us, even when we were dead in our transgressions, made us alive together with Christ (by grace you have been saved).

EPHESIANS 2:4-5 NASB

The kingdom of God works in ways that confound our minds. In our dying, we find life. In our suffering, we discover joy. In our weakness, we find strength. The traits of God's redemptive laws could go on.

There is no chasm too deep that Christ's undying affection does not reach it. Every part of our lives, every experience, is covered by his compassion. Today, let us come alive to the abundance of love's presence within and around us. Here we have all we need, not simply to just get by. We can thrive in the great mercy-tide of God's generous Spirit.

Merciful One, it is your great love that gives me strength to live when I have lost all motivation. You are the hand that holds me close in comfort, guides me steadily in grace, and strengthens me in faithful support. With you, I know that I will taste the sweetness of life again.

Tender Mercy

*His unforgettable works of surpassing wonder
reveal his grace and tender mercy.*
PSALM 111:4 TPT

All that God does is done in love. In the stripping-down seasons of our lives, it can be tempting to accuse God of cruelly leading us into lack. But God's ways are not marked by meanness or even apathy. He is full of loving care, leading us always in grace. His mercy is not harsh; it is tender.

Be quick to look for his fingerprint of mercy that brings healing. Watch for the evidence of his provision and his faithfulness. Even in the waiting, there is unbelievable grace in the presence of Holy Spirit, who never leaves you. Reach out and you will find that he is already close. His comfort surrounds you; open up and receive the peace that he offers today. Rest in relief.

God of mercy, fill me with the knowledge of your nearness today. I don't want to go on reliving past encounters with you; I need a fresh one. Meet me today with the presence of your perfect peace and give me eyes to see your mercy at work in my life. Do what only you can do.

Just a Crumb

Three things will last forever—
faith, hope, and love—
and the greatest of these is love.
1 Corinthians 13:13 NLT

There is no higher law than the law of God's perfect love. It is the very nature of his being. His affection cannot be tamed, and it will never be extinguished. The kindness of God's heart cannot be exaggerated, for we have only tasted but a crumb of it!

We will not go wrong when we set our lives to the rhythm of God's lovingkindness. We could try to outdo him in love, but we would never succeed. What a worthy pursuit: to try to out-love the very source of mercy. In our lives, we will find bountiful, beautiful blessings when we live as Christ did. We find life when we lay down our pride and choose to love others without expectation of anything in return.

Author of love, I choose to walk the path of your kindness. Though I try to test the limits of your love, I have not found the boundaries yet. You are so much better than any other love I've tasted; fill me with the purity of purpose found in your heart of affection.

Present Goodness

Let the wicked forsake their way, and the unrighteous their thoughts;
let them return to the LORD, that he may have mercy on them,
and to our God, for he will abundantly pardon.

ISAIAH 55:7 NRSV

It is never too late to return to the heart of your good Father. He is waiting with open arms whenever you are ready to run into them. It is true that your God never leaves you; that is a non-negotiable. But you get to decide whether you remain in the close fellowship of an open heart receiving his love as freely as he gives it.

Let today be the day you look to him again. He is closer than you know and full of all that you long for. His mercy meets you with exactly what you need in this moment. Find rest in the home of his love, and let your heart know once again that this is where you belong.

Faithful Father, I don't want to remain closed off to your love in any way today. I open up my heart to receive the revelation of your present goodness here and now. Wrap me up in your comfort and lift my head to see just how close you are.

Holy Help

The LORD will fight for you,
and you shall hold your peace.
EXODUS 14:14 NKJV

When battles rage in our lives, taking over our waking moments, it can be difficult to direct our energy into anything that is not of the moment. We become acutely aware of what is important to us and what is not: in relationships, in work, and in life.

When the demanding needs around us, as well as the crushing losses that we face, overwhelms our attention, what is our internal response? Is it to meet the needs in our own dwindling strength, or is it to lean into the support we have? May we always come back to this: the Lord will fight for us. His peace is our plentiful portion that can never be stolen. May we remember our God's ability to take care of everything, including us, all while covering us in his perfect peace.

Lord, I need your help more than I can express. I give up trying to hold things together on my own. When I feel I am falling apart, will you bind me in wholeness in your love? I will not resist your help today no matter how it comes. I trust you.

Gentle Care

Hear the voice of my pleas for mercy,
when I cry to you for help,
when I lift up my hands toward your most holy sanctuary.
PSALM 28:2 ESV

In the pit of despair, when darkness feels as though it is closing in around us, the Spirit of God is hemming us into his love. The Lord does not need to lean in closer to hear our whimpered cries, for he is already closer than we know. He hears even what is left unspoken.

The God who reads your heart is your present and constant help. There is not a thought that goes unnoticed by him. He does not hold your hurt against you. He washes over your seeping wounds with the salve of his compassionate healing presence. He is near, beloved. He is tending to you already; can you sense his gentle care?

Kind God, I am undone at the thought of your tenderness toward me. You know me so very well, and you meet me in ways that communicate the utmost care you have for me. Thank you. My despair unravels in your presence.

Opportunity for Grace

Do everything without grumbling or arguing, so that you may become blameless and pure, "children of God without fault in a warped and crooked generation." Then you will shine among them like stars in the sky as you hold firmly to the word of life.

PHILIPPIANS 2:14-16 NIV

There is an invitation, even in suffering, to practice laid-down love. Are we quick to argue when others don't see what we want them to? Are we prone to complain when our expectations are unmet? As God's people, we get to cast all of our frustrations at the feet of Jesus. May we walk in the wisdom of his Word that leads us into life.

Today, may we look at every hiccup in our plans as an opportunity to receive and extend grace. In getting to know why we react the way we do, we are able to offer compassion to both ourselves and to others. In receiving God's great mercy, we are empowered to forgive and seek forgiveness over and over again. Then we will shine as lovers of God who do not let pride keep us from loving well.

God over all, I need your grace to empower me to turn my offenses over to you. I know that you don't expect me to be perfect, so I'm laying down that impossible bar for myself. Let me be full of humility and grace. And when I am offended, help me to look within to see why without blaming others for my consternation.

Whole Self

May God himself, the God of peace, make you pure,
belonging only to him. May your whole self—spirit, soul, and body—
be kept safe and without fault when our Lord Jesus Christ comes.

1 THESSALONIANS 5:23 NCV

God's love is like an endless ocean. There are no limits to his merciful kindness. Why would we look for belonging anywhere else? There are no ropes we need to climb, hoops we need to jump through, or tests we need to ace in order to be completely accepted by him. We already are.

With that in mind, may we find ourselves coming to life in the light of God's pure affection to be who we were always meant to be. There is so much more to discover in the waters of his mercy, and we are already swimming in its depths. May we find ourselves whole in him through every season of the soul as we are being healed.

God of peace, you are the one who knows me better than any other: even better than I know myself. I trust that you will not stop leading me home to who you created me to be without the world's influences or demands. In the process, may I know your love in ways I had never imagined I would. You are worthy of all of me.

Cloud of Sorrow

*Rejoice, be made complete, be comforted, be like-minded, live in peace;
and the God of love and peace will be with you.*

2 CORINTHIANS 13:11 NASB

Do you feel like a fraction of your former self? Grief has a way of stripping us down to survival mode. You are not lost, and you are not broken. God is your healer, your comforter, and your faithful friend. This present sorrow has not depleted your life of joy. It is still there even though you may not see it as clearly.

There is a peace that comes with the pure presence of the Holy Spirit. God holds every part of us securely within his love. There is a solace that we find in the company of others who love us and who have also walked the road of suffering. We are not meant to ever go it alone in life. May we remain open to fellowship with God and others; they will help us see what we cannot see on our own for the cloud of sorrow surrounding us.

Holy Helper, I lean on your support to get me through this day. I know I can't do this alone, but I need your help to stay open to others in this time. Surround me with songs of deliverance not only through your help, but also through the hands of those around me.

Without Barriers

*He himself is our peace, who has made us both one
and has broken down in his flesh the dividing wall of hostility.*
EPHESIANS 2:14 ESV

There is absolutely nothing that stands between us and the love of God. No accusation of the enemy can nullify the truth of God's forever Word. Jesus is peace personified. He has made a way to the Father so we can know God in spirit and in truth without any barriers.

In the areas that we have felt small and stuck, there is an invitation to enter into the expanse of God's great wisdom. The presence of God's peace is both spacious and pervasive. There is no problem he cannot easily solve. Submit yourself to his love again and let the harmony of his heart fill yours with perfect peace.

Jesus, you are the one who tore the veil that separated mankind from the holiest place of God's presence. I know that your presence now dwells with me in the Holy Spirit, and I am so thankful that not even my biggest doubts or frustrations can keep me away from your overwhelming love. I let down the guard I have put around my heart and welcome you in; I want to walk in perfect peace today.

Law of Love

We were all baptized by one Spirit so as to form one body—
whether Jews or Gentiles, slave or free—
and we were all given the one Spirit to drink.
1 CORINTHIANS 12:13 NIV

When our preferences are offended and we find ourselves frustrated at those whom we are supposed to love unconditionally, what is our response? If we are looking simply through the lens of *me* and *my wants*, then offense will soon set in. But what have we been called to in the kingdom of God? How does his law of love work?

We receive unending, overflowing affection from a good Father who never wavers in love. He laid down his life in exceptional mercy and did not do it because of what was offered him. When we offer others compassion out of the overflow of God's kindness toward us, we must lay down the need for results. Let us love one another as Jesus taught us because we are a part of a diverse and beautiful family.

Father of love, I admit that I am quicker to judge than to try and understand those with a different lifestyle and viewpoint. But in my grief, I am learning that there is more that unifies us than divides us. Let me be aligned in your generous love that does not withhold based on what someone can offer me in return. You give freely, and I want to do the same.

Past the Galaxy

Great is your mercy, O LORD;
give me life according to your justice.
PSALM 119:156 NRSV

It can be so hard in the confinement of our experiences to remember that God's perspective is much bigger than our own. His mercy is larger than we could ever imagine. It reaches past our galaxy's end and keeps going into the endlessness of eternity. There is no beginning and there is no end to God's great love. The boundaries of our lives do not inhibit God one bit.

Instead of getting lost in the chaotic motion of your life today, will you submit your mind to God's perspective? Invite him to give you revelation to see from his vantage point. He doesn't miss a detail; you can trust him to lead you in love. You can trust him to wield justice in his perfect way and perfect timing.

Merciful One, I know that I only see a very small part of the greater reality in the world. I don't want to be limited in love today because of my limited perspective. Give me eyes to see how you see, so my heart may be opened to trust you more.

Greatest Victory

Every child of God defeats this evil world,
and we achieve this victory through our faith.

1 JOHN 5:4 NLT

There is no greater victory than the triumph of love's defeat over sin and death. In the resurrection power of Jesus, we live and breathe and have our being. There is nothing that we face today that Jesus did not already overcome; nothing is outside of the realm of his mercy.

There is power for you today in the grace that flows freely from God's throne. Jesus overcame the grave, and by his power you will overcome every scheme of the enemy with love and a sound mind. There is nothing in your life that God's loyal kindness has left untouched. Lay hold of that which Christ has already given you. You are an overcomer; you will get through this.

Great God, you are the one I set my life to. There is nothing that your resurrection power has not already touched. Help me see how I can stand in the power of your immensity in my life. Thank you that I am not helpless; you have given me everything I need.

Remarkable Presence

*"I will make all my goodness pass before you
and will proclaim before you my name 'The Lord.'
And I will be gracious to whom I will be gracious,
and will show mercy on whom I will show mercy."*

EXODUS 33:19 ESV

Do not fear: the Lord will come and he won't delay. In the wilderness of life, where we are tested by the elements, God does not leave us on our own. In our scarcity and our lack, God reveals himself in wonderful ways. When we aren't distracted by the noise of life, we are more apt to notice God's remarkable presence in mysterious ways.

Moses was fascinated by a burning bush that did not disintegrate. It captured his attention, the curiosity of it. And then God spoke. Are you disheartened by the barrenness of the desert you are walking through? Do not worry; God will reveal himself to you. He will do it.

Lord, I long for an encounter with you. Speak to me in the wilderness of my sorrow and let me know that you are with me. Do not delay in coming to me; I must know you more.

Every Generation

Know that the LORD your God, He is God, the faithful God who keeps covenant and mercy for a thousand generations with those who love Him and keep His commandments.

DEUTERONOMY 7:9 NKJV

The scope of God's mercy is so much larger than our little lives can contain. He is faithful and merciful to every generation as far back as mankind's origin. God will not let those he created and called by name be lost to the abyss of despair. He keeps his covenant of mercy to those who yield their lives to him in love.

Let our minds grow in understanding as our viewpoints expand in their perspective. May the revelation of the reach of God's love enlarge our hearts to receive more of his great affection. He will never let us go. He has not failed to fulfill his promise; he is faithful in working it all out. May we rest in the confidence of his ability. He surely will not forget a single vow he has made.

Faithful One, give me greater understanding of the enormity of your love today. Let my heart expand in its capacity to hold the revelations of your greatness toward all who submit their lives to you. I trust you!

Sweet Presence

Lord, answer me because your love is so good.
Because of your great kindness, turn to me.
PSALM 69:16 NCV

We could never exaggerate the lengths of God's love nor how sweet the taste of his presence is. He will never fail to answer our questions, our cries, and our longings with the kindness of his pure heart. He is so much better than we can imagine.

Submit all your wonderings to the Lord today. Every doubt, every curiosity, everything. He will answer you with the patience of a tender Father. He is so very gentle in his countenance toward you; you can trust him to care for you well even in conversation. Seek him today and be met by love once again.

Lord, I want to taste your goodness again today. I don't want to live as though I've forgotten your kindness. Remind me what it's like to be loved by you, and my heart will be filled with courage. Answer me as I turn toward you with an open heart.

Yes You Are

Once you were not a people, but now you are God's people;
once you had not received mercy, but now you have received mercy.
1 PETER 2:10 ESV

Do you ever wonder whether God will disown you? Even in your darkest days, in the pit of despair, you cannot escape his love. In submission or in rebellion, you are still his. His affection does not depend on your willingness to receive it. You are a child of a benevolent Father, and he won't ever stop loving you with a full and open heart.

It does not matter how you feel today; your identity as God's child is never called into question. Let him speak his words of life and truth over you, and soak in the kindness of his mercy once again. Let your mind be filled with the light of his truth. Let your heart be assured of the place you hold in his. Your Father loves you in unending measure, so don't disqualify yourself from his goodness today.

Good Father, I believe that I am who you say I am. As your child, I come to you in the reality of my weakness, and I rely on you to speak your words of life over me again. Remind me of what you see when you look at me and how you created me to thrive.

Wealth of Wisdom

Guide me in your truth and teach me,
for you are God my Savior,
and my hope is in you all day long.

PSALM 25:5 NIV

There is a wealth of wisdom in the heart of your Father waiting to be discovered through fellowship with his Spirit. Whatever it is that you lack, he has in abundance. Whatever your question, he has an answer. There is no problem that you face that he does not have a perfect, timely solution to.

You can trust that he knows best. You have access to his truth that makes wise the simple, causes the lame to walk, and sets the prisoner free! Let your racing thoughts settle and turn your attention to the only wise God. Commune with your Creator today.

All-knowing One, my mind has been searching for answers to the questions of my heart. Will you meet with me today in your goodness and calm my anxious thoughts? Give me your wisdom that offers solutions to even the most complex problems. I need you!

Burrow In

The LORD is near to all who call on him,
yes, to all who call on him in truth.
PSALM 145:18 NLT

Grief feels like a narrow tunnel, where everything unnecessary is pushed to the side. We walk, step by step, through the confinement of our suffering. And yet, it is in this place that we are actually tucked into the mercy heart of God. Our sorrow and pain is close, but the love of God is even closer.

He is near. Do you feel alone in your loss? He is close. Do you struggle to get out of bed some mornings? He is the blanket over you. There is no need to press in closer, for he is already with you. Burrow in deeper if you must. Just know that he is so very near.

Lord, when I feel closed in by my grief, remind me that I am already hemmed in by your love. You wrap around me like a warm blanket, tucking me tight into your compassion. I am yours, and you are my greatest comfort.

The Expert

Lift your hands and give thanks to God
for his marvelous kindness
and for his miracles of mercy for those he loves!
PSALM 107:8 TPT

Think about the kindest, most generous and caring person you know. How does it feel to be in their presence? What is it like to be loved by them? Now consider that God's compassionate character is infinitely greater. He is pure in motive, expert in delivery, and always, always loving. He doesn't make any mistakes and he will never let you down.

God lavishes miracles of mercy on those he loves. You are the object of his extravagant affection! There is not a moment where he lifts his hand of mercy from your life. Not even one. He is the expert at bringing restoration to desolate places and redeeming that which was lost. You can trust him today. He is full of goodness still.

Kind God, you are the maker of heaven and earth and you created me. Your revelations of kindness are like refreshing waters to my soul. They are like bursts of cool wind on a hot summer's day. You are the one I look to today for hope. I trust you to keep working out your love in my life.

Nothing to Offer

It depends not on human will or exertion,
but on God, who has mercy.
ROMANS 9:16 ESV

Are you tired of trying your best only to realize you don't have enough to give in this season? Your worth is not tied to your productivity. Your ability to rest is not dependent upon what you've accomplished. When you have nothing to offer, God comes in with the same amount of great grace as he does when you are at your best.

God's mercy is never dependent upon us: not our reception of it, recognition of it, or what we can offer in return. It is an outflow of God's very nature. Let us receive his mercy with open hearts and lives, no matter how inept we feel. He is better—so much better—than we can ever give him credit for.

God of mercy, you are so rich in love. I give up trying to earn it; I know I never could, and what's more, that's not what you want from me. I want to be so full of love that I live as the confident child of God you created me to be. Though I have nothing to offer you today but my time and attention, I give it to you.

Unending River

Oh, give thanks to the Lord, for He is good!
For His mercy endures forever.
1 CHRONICLES 16:34 NKJV

From sunrise to sunset, to the moon and stars and the cycle of the same, God's mercy endures forever. His love is an unending river of pleasures to those who swim in its depths. Why would we look for satisfaction anywhere else? He is the sustainer of every living thing, and he is the redeemer of all that has been lost.

God is as worthy of thanks today as he always was. He is the God of triumphant breakthrough, and he is the God who sits with us, wrapping us in his comfort, when we are brokenhearted. He is the rescuer of the needy and the healer of the broken. He is generous in kindness and so very slow to anger. He is worthy of our trust today and always.

Provider, you are so very good to me. I remember the ways you have led me in love and truth in my life, and how you've shown your incredible mercy. I won't forget that you are a good God. Thank you for your patience with me and your unending kindness toward me.

Good Gifts

Grace, mercy and peace will be with us, from God the Father and from Jesus Christ, the Son of the Father, in truth and love.

2 JOHN 1:3 NASB

God is a Father who gives generously from his storehouse. He offers the mercy of his heart to all who look to him. He does not give stones when his children ask for bread. He does not play cruel jokes on his kids and bid them to get over it. He is full of kindness in every moment, offering just what we need. Where he is, there is comfort, joy, peace, and belonging.

The fruit of the Spirit are all evidence of his life in us. Where there is strife, there is an invitation for God's merciful nature to meet us. Where there is sorrow, there is comfort to be found in his loving embrace. Find what you need in the presence of God today.

Faithful Father, will you meet me with the goodness of your heart today? I long to know your love in deep, fresh ways. You know what I need, and I trust you to fill my longings.

Ring Loudly

I have tried hard to find you—
don't let me wander from your commands.
PSALM 119:10 NLT

Jesus' words echo strongly in the devotion of the hearts of those who look for him: seek and you will find. There is honor in knocking on heaven's door, looking for the answers to questions that ring loudly in your heart. You will find what you are looking for.

God is very near, and he is a trustworthy guide through the different terrains of this life. You can trust his merciful heart to lead you in his goodness all the days of your life. You will not be put to shame in his presence, and you won't go without in your day of need. Trust him; he is for you!

Holy Spirit, guide me along the river of living water where I will find refreshment for my soul. I have been journeying the dry and dusty road of disappointment and heartache; revive me with your waters of mercy! Lead me on in love; I won't stop seeking after you.

Fires of Testing

In Your great mercy
You did not utterly consume them nor forsake them;
For You are God, gracious and merciful.

NEHEMIAH 9:31 NKJV

We cannot escape the flames of the fires of testing when they come. Grief leads us into the fire that will purify us; we will not be destroyed! God is with us in it. He will not let us be consumed but will use the heat of our suffering to remove the impurities of old, worn-out ways that no longer serve us.

May we trust God in the process. We are not alone. He covers us in the oil of his mercy that acts as a salve to our wounds in the midst of the pressure of great sorrow. He will never abandon us to be devoured by our circumstances. May we not believe the lies that tempt us to think that he has forsaken us. He never, ever will!

Gracious God, I can't pretend that I have never thought "Where are you?" in the middle of my suffering, but I believe that your mercy and faithfulness are true. Reveal your presence in my life again today and encourage my heart as I meditate on your nearness.

Now Word

God is able to bless you abundantly, so that in all things at all times,
having all that you need, you will abound in every good work.
2 CORINTHIANS 9:8 NIV

Have you been living on the gifts of last season? There is nothing wrong with enjoying what you have been given, but there is always more in the heart of the Father for you. He is a generous God, and he always meets you where you are, not where you've been.

There is a "now" word that he has for you—a revelation that is precisely for this moment in your life. There is no need to relive the highlights of yesterday in order to keep your faith strong. He wants fellowship with you. Will you press into the heart of God and hear his voice today? He is speaking. Lean in.

Generous God, I have been cruising through these days clinging onto the gifts of yesterday. I know that you say there is abundance in your love. Will you meet me with your very present help today?

Swept Into Peace

I had said in my alarm,
"I am cut off from your sight."
But you heard the voice of my pleas for mercy
when I cried to you for help.

PSALM 31:22 ESV

When despair sets in, fear races us onto the road of anxiety. It moves quickly, and without the anchor of peace, we can find ourselves caught in a whirlwind of what-ifs and how-comes. God never rushes us with chaotic concern. His ways and voice are marked by the peace and space they bring.

The Lord hears our every cry for help. He is not slow to come to our aid; it's that fear has sped up our systems to think we have missed something along the way. When his love comes in like a rushing river, it sweeps us up into its calm and steady path. There is space to rest and breathe. All we need to do is call out to him and he is there to take the reins of our hearts once more and lead us along his path of peace.

Good God, come to my aid again. Slow down my racing thoughts as I submit them to you. Drive the chaos of fear away with your powerful love. Thank you!

Resurrection Life

If while we were still enemies,
God fully reconciled us to himself through the death of his Son,
then something greater than friendship is ours.
Now that we are at peace with God,
and because we share in his resurrection life,
how much more we will be rescued from sin's dominion!
ROMANS 5:10 TPT

There is resurrection life in the power of Jesus. It is not reserved for some far-off day; it is ours now through fellowship with the Holy Spirit. We have peace with God no matter what our circumstances are in the moment. The trials and pain of this life do not negate the greater hope we have.

It is in our weakness that we experience the extensive strength of God. Jesus reigns victorious over every foe; he has already defeated death. In this same resurrection power we experience the abundant life of his kingdom on earth as it is in heaven. Though we see only in part, we catch glimpses of his glory, how he weaves everything together with the thread of his marvelous mercy.

Jesus, you are the resurrection and the life. Fill me with your love and give me eyes to see your power at work in my life in the right here and now. I rely on you, Triumphant One!

Constant Conversation

Let us then with confidence draw near to the throne of grace,
that we may receive mercy and find grace to help in time of need.
HEBREWS 4:16 ESV

In the morning and the evening, and all the moments in-between, may we find ourselves continually turning to our heavenly Father in constant conversation. There is help whenever we need it. Are we not seeing things clearly? Let us look to him for his perspective. Are we struggling to forgive someone? Let's ask him for grace to heal and forgive.

There is confidence in close companionship. Those we know best we turn to with our real selves. Do we have this kind of relationship with God? If not, now is as good a time as any to get to know how faithful he is. Let's give him our whole selves, not a manufactured version. He wants us as we are.

Father, draw near to me. Through your Spirit, will you speak to me throughout my day? I want to know you as you are, not what I expect you to be. Show me your goodness that knows no end. I want deep friendship with you.

July

He will answer the prayers of the needy;

he will not reject their prayers.

PSALM 102:17 NCV

Refreshing Tide

To the LORD our God belong mercy and forgiveness,
though we have rebelled against Him.

DANIEL 9:9 NKJV

In the places of our deep need, we can easily be overwhelmed by the scarcity we perceive. If we were on our own, perhaps worry would be warranted. But we are never alone. The Lord is better than the fleeting satisfaction of temporary pleasures. He is constant in love and abundant in mercy at all times.

God's goodness is better than the most valuable treasure we could imagine. He is rich in kindness, and we are never without it. Whatever it is that we face today, God's compassion is a river of life that flows freely into our lives. May we wash ourselves in the waters of his presence. In this refreshing tide, we will find our souls revived. He is our source of life today and always.

Lord my God, you are the only hope I have left when my world spins. I know there is more life in you than I have yet experienced, and I want to be revived in your living waters of mercy today. Flow over my mind and remove the dust of my disappointment.

Carry Me

Your words have comforted those who fell,
and you have strengthened those who could not stand.
JOB 4:4 NCV

In the arms of our loving Father, we have the support we need to get through any circumstance. He carries us when our legs give out, and he comforts us when our hearts break. He doesn't grow tired of our need, and he won't ever ridicule our dependence on him. Dependence is what he encourages!

Even when we venture on our own path, we have Wisdom's words to guide and correct us. We are never without Love's presence in our lives. He is our source, our strength, and our faithful friend. Whether we run or crawl, may we do it with the confidence of a child aiming toward their Father's arms. And when we cannot move, he is there to pick us up.

Good Father, you are the one who holds my heart together when it feels as though it's shattered. In your comforting embrace, I know that you will heal every wound and encourage me to keep going when I am ready to walk on my own two feet again. But right now, I rest in your support and care, letting you carry me.

Mourning Allowed

*"Blessed are the poor in spirit, for theirs is the kingdom of heaven.
Blessed are those who mourn, for they will be comforted."*
MATTHEW 5:3-4 NIV

There is no escape from pain in life. What would it be like if we were so well attuned to the reality of God's nearness, that when suffering came, we would not question his goodness? Pain is not an indicator of punishment; we have to realize this. It is a sign that something is not right.

Just as we would not ignore a protruding bone in our body, but seek medical assistance, we should not ignore the pain of grief. There is a healing process, and recognition is an important part of this. Jesus said, "Blessed are those who mourn, for they will be comforted." If we let ourselves mourn, we will know the comfort of God. May we call on our healer as often as needed.

Comforter, I don't want to prolong my healing process. I will not ignore the weight of my sorrow today, but I bring it all to you. Healer, heal me. Teacher, teach me. Give me comfort for my mourning today.

Pathways of Peace

"Because of the tender mercy of our God,
With which the Sunrise from on high will visit us,
To shine upon those who sit in darkness and the shadow of death,
To guide our feet into the way of peace."
LUKE 1:78-79 NASB

When we sit in the darkness of a grief-stricken night, unable to see anything around us, our God is a shining light of peace. We are not alone in our sorrow, not even for a moment. Mercy surrounds us; even when we cannot sense it, it is our constant covering.

The Lord, in his comfort, will lead us in pathways of peace. We won't need to fumble forward, for he is our strong support and he won't let us fall. He lifts us out of the pit of our despair and places our feet on the firm foundation of his lovingkindness. He holds us up with his strong arm of faithfulness. He won't let us go.

My God, I wait on you today. I need the light of your presence to shine on my heart. Reveal where you are as I trust that you are nearer than I know. Lead me in the peace of your presence and revive my weary heart today in your love.

Flowing Fountain

"I am the Alpha and the Omega—the Beginning and the End. To all who are thirsty I will give freely from the springs of the water of life."

REVELATION 21:6 NLT

Are you thirsty for more vibrant life today? There is a flowing fountain of mercy in the presence of God. Ask, and you will receive. Seek and you will find what you're looking for. Drink deeply today of God's present grace that is more than enough to satisfy your soul.

You have the Spirit of the living God with you. You have access to the deep wells of his faithful love. Will you deny yourself the refreshing you will surely find in his presence? Do not hold back in your asking or your receiving. He does not withhold even a bit of his affection from you today. Lean in, and you will see that he is already closer than you expected.

Alpha and Omega, you encompass all of time and space, and still you care about me. I am undone and still so hungry for more of you. Fill me with the revelation of your Word that my heart may taste and be satisfied in your goodness.

Met in the Mess

Magnify the marvels of your mercy to all who seek you.
Make your Pure One wonderful to me,
like you do for all those who turn aside
to hide themselves in you.

PSALM 17:7 TPT

As you look for God's goodness in your life, you will find it. Though you may struggle to see the evidence of mercy's fingerprint in your darkest hours, you will not be able to deny love's mark on your life when the light of his glory shines on you. You will see treasures and gardens of glory where once you thought there was only barrenness. He will let nothing in your life go to waste.

Hide yourself in God's great heart of compassion; there is room for you and all of your baggage. He consistently uplifts the humble and holds close the crushed in spirit. There is no need to dress yourself up to dwell in him. Don't worry; even in your questioning, he holds you near. You cannot be moved from his grace. His mercy meets you in your mess.

Pure One, as I hide myself in your constant nature, I trust that you will take good care of me. May I know the awe and wonder of beholding you in your glory when my eyes open in the light of your presence. As I wait, mold my heart with your peace.

Solidarity

Blessed be the God and Father of our Lord Jesus Christ,
the Father of mercies and God of all comfort,
who comforts us in all our affliction
so that we will be able to comfort those who are in any affliction
with the comfort with which we ourselves are comforted by God.

2 CORINTHIANS 1:3-4 NASB

The experience of loss is lonely, and yet it is universal. When we walk through the valley of the shadow of death, we are marked forever. When we recognize those who tread the familiar path, we can offer the relief we've received and the solidarity of understanding.

Your suffering is not in vain. In the intensity of your sorrow, God himself is your comfort and your strength. He is close, and he is full of love. Still, there are others who know this walk well. Let the solace of those who have walked this path before be a comfort and a support. When you are through the worst of it, you will do the same.

Comforter, I rely on you in ways I cannot even begin to verbalize to anyone else. And yet, I know that I am not alone in the pain. May my heart find comfort in you and in the support of those who have walked this road before me.

Unparalleled Wisdom

The wisdom from above is first pure, then peaceable, gentle, open to reason, full of mercy and good fruits, impartial and sincere.
JAMES 3:17 ESV

The wisdom of God is without parallel in the earth. Though we have strategies and plans, they don't compare to the breadth of God's understanding. Though we are constantly learning more insights both in the world around us and within ourselves, they are but a tiny glimpse into the knowledge of God.

Why do we search for understanding in what we can see, when the one who set the earth in motion and the planets in orbit, is the one who calls us his children? Wisdom is our counselor. Pure truth is our companion. It is full of peace, gentle in its leading, open to seeing other's points of view, and full of sincerity. May we press into the wonderful wisdom of our great God and King who sees all, is in all, and loves all.

Wise God, I come to you seeking answers for my many questions. Your solutions are incomparable to those I could find in the world. I rely on you for the peace-loving resolutions that my life so desperately needs. Lead me in your matchless understanding.

Eyes on You

You do see! Indeed you note trouble and grief,
that you may take it into your hands;
the helpless commit themselves to you;
you have been the helper of the orphan.

PSALM 10:14 NRSV

God not only sees you, but he cares for you in a way that exceeds the love of anyone you've ever known. He is full of kindness toward you, helping you whenever you can't find your way. He is Father to the fatherless, the healer of the broken, and a helper to the helpless.

He sees you in your trouble and in your grief. He lifts your head so you see that his eye is already on you. You don't have to do more in this moment; just lift your eyes to your present help and rescuer. He is already working things together for your good. He will never let you be lost to despair. He is your holy hope, and he is holding you.

Savior, you have not let go of me yet. Help me to see you at work in the chaos of my life. You will bring peace and rest, and I will taste your goodness as you feed me from your hand. Revive my hope again today.

Shedding the Old

Sow for yourselves righteousness;
Reap in mercy;
Break up your fallow ground,
For it is time to seek the LORD,
Till He comes and rains righteousness on you.
HOSEA 10:12 NKJV

In the throes of grief, it can feel as if we're losing ourselves. But we cannot be lost, not really. In the shedding of old skins—the way things were—the underlying layer can feel raw and vulnerable, but it allows us to experience the world in new ways. Seek the Lord today, and don't stop looking for the evidence of his faithfulness in your life.

The same God of comfort who was with you yesterday is generous in love today. He will lead you in joy once again. His plans for you have not changed though your own may have shifted course. Take hope in the constancy of his powerful mercy that never lets up.

Lord, today I come to you with all my raw emotion and vulnerability that leaves me feeling unsure about so many things in life. Fuel my faith today and rain your righteousness on me so no matter what is left in question, you are not one of those things.

The Safe Place

Even though I walk through the darkest valley,
I will fear no evil, for you are with me;
your rod and your staff, they comfort me.

PSALM 23:4 NIV

The dark valley of suffering can feel as suffocating as a coffin and, at the same time, as perilous as a lone journey into the wilderness. There is good news for those of us journeying along the miserable path of grief: we are not alone. God is our shepherd, keeping us close and safe when we don't know where we're going. He is our guide, leading us with confidence, for he sees everything that is around and ahead of us.

Even though we are filled with deep sorrow that cannot be summed up in words, we don't need to be afraid of what will become of us. We are held in the Redeemer's arms and kept in love's gaze. When everything falls apart, he does not. He is our safe place, and his nearness is our comfort.

Good Shepherd, you lead me faithfully with your love. Though I struggle to see clearly for the grief that fogs my mind, I know that you are near. Comfort me today with your love and cause any dread in my heart to flee. You are good and you have not changed.

In the Depths

> *"I have seen what they have done,*
> *but I will heal them.*
> *I will guide them and comfort them*
> *and those who felt sad for them.*
> *They will all praise me."*
>
> ISAIAH 57:18 NCV

What needs do you have today? Which areas of your life need the healing touch of the Comforter? There is no need too great that your Creator and Savior cannot meet. Let your heart take hope that he sees you just as you are and he is ready to reach out in fullness of love.

The oil of God's presence is a healing salve to the wounded heart. Open up and receive it. Let this be the day where you lay aside your doubt and your expectation of limitation and invite God to move in ways that only he can. He is moving already; will you press in for more?

Healer, I need you more than I can express. Meet me in the depths of my pain; I give you full access to my heart. Speak to me, for I am listening. Touch me, and I will be healed.

A Complex Song

My loving God, the harp in my heart will praise you.
Your faithful heart toward us will be the theme of my song.
Melodies and music will rise to you, the Holy One of Israel.
PSALM 71:22 TPT

When our lives are woven into the heart of God, the theme of our existence is the very nature of God. His faithfulness is the song; his mercy is the melody. God's unfailing love is both the rhythm and the bass. Its tune never grows old, and it somehow evolves into greater complexity as our lives develop.

If we listen for it, we will hear it: the sound of his goodness that has always been playing over our lives. The song has not changed though we may struggle to recognize it through the commotion of our anguish. This will not last. The chaotic noise of grief will settle until we hear the telltale melody of our faithful God playing through our darkest moments.

Creator, you are the orchestrator of my life. You take even the most off-pitch areas and redirect them until they are like a solo that started out questionable and found its way back to the right key and meter. There is nothing you cannot do. Quiet the clamoring noise; I want to hear your song play over my life.

Greater Liberty

I prayed to the LORD, and he answered me.
He freed me from all my fears.
Those who look to him for help will be radiant with joy.

PSALM 34:4-5 NLT

Freedom is not a vain pursuit; it is what Christ intended for us. Wherever we are hemmed in by limitations that God never meant for us, there is an opportunity to experience greater liberty in him. There is no end to the great love he gives us—a love that provides confidence and joy to live in unrestricted fellowship with him.

Where does your life align in God's love? You will know it by the freedom from fear, shame, and doubt: the areas that are unhindered in connection to the source of life. Where are you bound to fear? Ask God to free you from this today and watch how he answers you.

God of my liberty, you are so good to me. I offer you the places of my life where fear and shame still reign and ask that you would set me free. I long to live in greater freedom in you. Deliver me, my Savior!

Not a Limited Resource

May the Lord of peace himself give you peace at all times and in every way. The Lord be with all of you.

2 THESSALONIANS 3:16 NIV

When was the last time you felt peace wash over your heart, mind, and soul? Whether it was an hour ago, a year ago, or longer, it does not matter. This moment, right here and now, is an invitation to receive the peace of God that comforts, revives and keeps you.

May the Lord of peace himself give you his perfect peace to meet your needs in every way, in every moment. He is already with you. His Spirit dwells within you. Take a deep breath, close your eyes, and tune into the deep place of connection where spirit meets Spirit. May peace flood your being as you do.

Peace Giver, I am so thankful that your presence never goes to waste. Your peace is not a limited resource reserved for my worst moments but the boundless atmosphere that covers me all the days of my life. Where I have struggled to sense you, wrap around me with your tangible presence once again.

My Only Defense

I will sing of Your power;
Yes, I will sing aloud of Your mercy in the morning;
For You have been my defense
And refuge in the day of my trouble.

PSALM 59:16 NKJV

The Lord God your creator is also the one who defends you. Have you grown tired of pleading your case to those who don't seem to care? Let your forever advocate take it up! He will not let you be taken out by the schemes of the enemy. His truth stands firm, and no lie will hold up when he speaks on your behalf.

Rest in him today and trust him to do what only he can do. Let go of the nagging need for others to understand you when you've done your best; be true and be loving. Everything else is out of your hands. Don't worry; rather take refuge in the safety of God's thoughts toward you.

Defender, I give up the anxiety of trying to get others to understand me. You know me better than anyone. I trust you to work all things out in your way and your time. I hide myself in your love today.

Mercy Nature

Be mindful of your mercy, O LORD,
and of your steadfast love,
for they have been from of old.
PSALM 25:6 NRSV

The love of God is the essence of his very being. It is timeless, having no beginning or end. It has always been the pathway to connection; there is nothing else like it in all the world. The Lord will never forget to act in mercy toward his people because mercy is his nature.

Do you feel as if you're lost in the middle of a sea of sorrow with no view of the shore? The Lord is your ship, your rudder, and the wind in your sails. He will never let you drift from his great grace. Rest today in the knowledge that he is with you, he is for you, and you are safe in his love.

Merciful Lord, you could never forget your mercy and love for they are as ancient and timeless as you are. I lean into the sanctuary of your affectionate heart today. Let my soul find rest here.

There Is More

> *He who sits on the throne said,*
> *"Behold, I am making all things new."*
> *And He said, "Write, for these words are faithful and true."*
> REVELATION 21:5 NASB

Everything is made new in Jesus. He's constantly redeeming and restoring that which is lost and broken. His fingerprints of mercy are all over our lives. There is nothing out of the realm of his resurrection power. He is life, and he is breathing new life into us even now.

There is always more in the kingdom of God; it is a kingdom of abundance. There is more healing, more wisdom, more love, more power. There is more. In the areas of our lives where we look and see lack, let us invite the Spirit of God to give us his perspective. He is making all things new; it's what he does.

Faithful One, you never stop bringing life out of ashes. Give me eyes to see where new life is blooming out of the ruins of loss. Renew my hope in you today.

Not Okay

He was despised and rejected by men,
a man of sorrows and acquainted with grief;
and as one from whom men hide their faces he was despised,
and we esteemed him not.

ISAIAH 53:3 ESV

In the depths of our grief, there is one who knows what we are experiencing better than any other. Jesus experienced humanity in its fullness; he was well acquainted with the same challenges and heartaches we face. He is not removed from our suffering. He knows it well because he lived it.

Have you kept God at a distance in your grief because you felt like he just couldn't understand? Perhaps today is the day to look at his experience of loss and heartbreak. Invite him into the depths of your sadness. He is not indifferent toward you. He feels what you feel, and he enters into mourning with you. There is no rush to get to the place where you feel okay. He doesn't expect you to shake this off. Let him share it with you. Even in your suffering, he is with you.

Jesus, sometimes I forget that you're familiar with every aspect of my humanity. You lived it as well. Comfort me with your presence; I'm listening to what you have to say today.

Thread of Grace

Everything that was written in the past was written to teach us.
The Scriptures give us patience and encouragement
so that we can have hope.
ROMANS 15:4 NCV

The Word of God is full of wisdom for us to fill up on. When we forget the character of God, can we not look into the Scriptures and find the thread of his grace sewn into each story? There is encouragement for us in seeing how he came through time and again in his faithfulness toward his people.

God's faithful love leaps off the pages of the Scriptures and encourages our hearts. Let us learn from those who came before us and let us follow the example of those who loved God with all their hearts, souls, and minds. More than anything, we are meant for relationship. Take some time to read the Word today and be encouraged by the nature of our constantly compassionate God.

Living Word, I look to your life to know what you are really like. I long to know your presence more intimately; I want to walk with you like those I read about in the Scriptures. Lead me further into your love as I learn more about your incredible mercy in the lives of your people.

Intense Love

Lord, you know the hopes of the helpless.
Surely you will hear their cries and comfort them.
PSALM 10:17 NLT

In the desperate cries of our deepest needs, God hears us and meets us with his great mercy. He does not delay in flooding in with the rushing river of his love. He is faithful to help us whenever we need it. He is constant to cover us in his compassion. His love is jealous for us. It is more powerful than the grave and deeper than the most intense pain we experience.

He knows the hopes of the helpless. Where we have reached the end of our rope and our very last bit of courage, there he is with comfort and strength. He works everything out for the good of those who love him. He will not let us be lost to the crushing pain of heartbreak. He is near; he is here.

Lord, you know the deep pain in my heart. Meet me in it now with your close comfort. I need you more than I can express. Turn to me and I will live.

In Equal Measure

*Our fathers who were delivered from Egypt
didn't fully understand your wonders,
and they took you for granted.
Over and over you showed them
such tender love and mercy!*

PSALM 106:7 TPT

God does not withhold his love from us no matter what we are walking through. When Moses led the Israelites from their captivity in Egypt into the wilderness where they depended on God's presence to guide and sustain them, there was a tangible presence of need and an equal measure of provision. With a cloud by day and a pillar of fire by night, God led them.

There was manna for their bellies straight from heaven. They always had what they needed, and God did not stop showing his love and mercy toward them. In the same way, God guides and provides for us today. He will not let us go hungry, and he won't leave us to wander. He is the source of everything we need today and forever.

Merciful Father, you never stop providing for your children. May I rest in the confidence of your leadership in my life, able to stand in your goodness and your faithfulness. You never change; I am secure in your love.

Calming Compassion

You who are my Comforter in sorrow,
my heart is faint within me.
JEREMIAH 8:18 NIV

Let the Comforter wrap around your weary heart today with the tangible presence of his love. He is full of peace to keep you and compassion to calm your racing thoughts. Give him your worry and receive the rest of his mercy. He is faithful to guard you in his love.

Do not hesitate to cry out when you need him. His ready help is at your side with strength to support you. You are not alone. He kneels with you in the dust of your broken dreams and whispers words of love to knit the fraying edges of hope into the fabric of his redemption plan. You can trust him. He has you.

Comforter, hold me close in your arms of love today. Strengthen me as I lean back in your mercy. I rest in you, knowing that I need not do anything more today to earn your help or attention. You are my help; draw nearer still.

Come Alive

*He will take our weak mortal bodies
and change them into glorious bodies like his own,
using the same power with which he will bring
everything under his control.*
PHILIPPIANS 3:21 NLT

In the resurrection power of Christ, we stand. It is in this grave-busting might that we rise, we move, and we come alive to the kingdom of God on earth as it is in heaven. There is nothing that can overpower it; no enemy or force could cancel its strength.

When God's kingdom ushers us into the coming age of his rule and reign, this power will change our bodies so they will not decay or decline. We will live forever with the King of glory as our sun and shield. Death's sting will become a memory, and the pain of heartbreak and sorrow will be forever healed. We see but through a glass dimly, but then we will see clearly.

All-powerful One, your love is stronger than death. In your power, I will rise in glory, just as you did when you rose from the grave. I long for the day when everything is clear. In the meantime, I will trust in you and watch as your power moves mountains in my life.

Flesh and Spirit

To set the mind on the flesh is death,
but to set the mind on the Spirit is life and peace.
ROMANS 8:6 ESV

The flesh represents that which is temporary in life. When we focus all our attention on it, there will inevitably be disappointment and discouragement. The Spirit represents all that is eternal. When we focus on that which does not change, we will find that we are filled with the hope that accompanies it.

There is life and peace in our spirits fellowshipping with God's Spirit. He feeds us with the life-giving strength of his truth. What is the fruit of our thoughts? Surely we can see the evidence of what we are giving our time and attention to. Today, let us set our minds on things above—the things that never change. God is faithful in love both now and forever.

Holy Spirit, as I turn my attention toward you today, fill me with the fruit of your Word. Let the peace of your presence flood my mind, washing over every fear, doubt, and discouragement. I know your ways are better than mine, and I want to walk in your steps instead of treading my own path.

Saturated

I will be glad and rejoice in Your mercy,
For You have considered my trouble;
You have known my soul in adversities.
PSALM 31:7 NKJV

One of the most beautiful things about God is that he is as near to us in our despair as he is in our delight. He knows us so very well— better than our most trusted friend. He sees what no one else can see, straight through our outer layers into the depths of our hearts.

He knows our worries and our longings. He sees our weaknesses and our strengths. He doesn't hold a thing against us; he always leads us in love. We can trust his heart to guide us in kindness all the days of our lives. He is a good, good Father.

Father, you see me where I am today; you know the state of my heart. Consider my trouble and lift me out of the pit of my anguish. I need your healing touch again. Lean in, Lord, with your love that fills in every crack. Saturate me in your extravagant affection.

Ask for More

*May mercy, peace, and love
be yours in abundance.*
JUDE 1:2 NRSV

When we're looking for our needs to be met, how often do we think, "If only…?" The bare minimum would suffice, right? But God does not dole his love out in ways that simply satisfies the minimal expectation. He is full of abundance for every season of the soul. There's more than enough to go around.

We cannot exhaust God's mercy; it is ever increasing in its flow. God will never run out of his peace to impart to us. Think about what it's like to be deprived of something and then to have it in your life again. You do not scantily partake; you eat as much as you can! God will give you enough to not only satisfy your craving, but to sustain you. Don't hesitate to ask for more.

Generous God, too often I'm just looking for you to meet my need as it is. Rarely do I expect a generous portion of more than I could think to ask for. Isn't that what you're like? You are an abundant provider for every need in every situation. I'm asking you to meet me with your abundant provision today. Go above and beyond my expectations in accordance with your character.

Soul Intuition

May the God who gives us his peace and wholeness be with you all.
Yes, Lord, so let it be!

ROMANS 15:33 TPT

In your search for wholeness, where has it led you? Has it led you further from yourself to experts who sound like they know what they're talking about? Or has it led you back to yourself? You already have access to everything you need to heal and be whole. You have fellowship with the Spirit of wisdom.

Following another's leading in life does nothing for you if it does not point you back to what you already have right here and now. Tune in to the intuition of your soul that knows the tender voice of your Father. Ask the Holy Spirit to give you wisdom and insight; there is no lack of availability with God. There are no waiting lists or requirements to meet. Here, now, find your fulfillment in fellowship with him.

Holy Spirit, I'm so grateful that I have you to guide me into truth. According to your Word, lead me in your kindness and fill me with the fruit of your presence. Oh, how I long for the joy, peace, and love that you give. I find true wholeness in you.

New Once More

That faith and that knowledge come from the hope for life forever,
which God promised to us before time began.
TITUS 1:2 NCV

In the cycle of life, we may find ourselves looking for hope in different areas. Will we get the job? Will we have kids? Will we get the all-clear? There is one hope that is rooted in the rich soil of God's faithful love; will we live after this life is done?

May we be encouraged today in the truth of God's trustworthy love that broke the power of death through Jesus' resurrection. We too will be raised from the confines of these limited bodies and be made new once more for all eternity. God will do all that he said he will, and we will live forever with him in glory.

Faithful One, encourage my heart in the truth of your promises. I wait for the fulfillment of every hope, but the hope for eternal life more than any other. As I continue to watch your faithfulness work in my life, may it convince me more and more of the coming hope of life forever with you!

Tears Counted

*Those who sow in tears
shall reap with shouts of joy.*
PSALM 126:5 ESV

God takes your tears and uses them to water the garden of your heart. They do not fall to the ground wasted. Every tear is counted though its significance may remain a mystery to you. You will see, when this season passes and another arrives, that God uses what we forget about to coax sweet fruit from the vines of our lives.

Nothing is wasted, certainly not your sorrow. God has not forgotten you, his child. He holds you close in the comfort of his love and soothes you until your heart rate matches the rhythm of his own. Do not despair; you are not alone. The Holy Spirit is within you and working in your life.

God, I trust that you will use my heartbreak and sorrow to lead me into deeper realms of joy. Let me taste the sweet fruit of your faithfulness toward me. Today, open my eyes to see where you meet me in my present grief.

Tethered Hopes

We can make our plans,
but the LORD determines our steps.

PROVERBS 16:9 NLT

When we have reached the end of our abilities, do we trust God to lead us in love? When our plans fall apart, do we despair, or do we tether our hopes to the faithfulness of our good Father? We can move toward our designs for our lives, but that does not mean that life will align with our strategies.

God, however, is full of wisdom and insight into every situation. He leads us in mercy even when it doesn't look the way we had hoped. He knows what he is doing. We can trust that his plans for us are better than what we could throw together on our own. He is infinitely good, and his intentions are full of kindness.

Lord, I trust that you see what I cannot see; you will not stop leading me in your compassion. I bind my heart to yours, and I let go of how I thought things should be. Help me to release my disappointments to you and trust that I will taste your goodness in my life again.

August

I am praying to you
because I know you will answer, O God.
Bend down and listen as I pray.

PSALM 17:6 NLT

Attentive

"People everywhere seem to worry about making a living, but your heavenly Father knows your every need and will take care of you."
LUKE 12:30 TPT

When we look at the demands of our lives and can't see how we will meet them with our own resources, it is easy to get overwhelmed. God does not shame us for our lack or demand that we figure things out on our own. He is a good and faithful Father, always providing for his children no matter what the need is.

When was the last time your heart truly rested in the faithfulness of God? He knows you better than you know yourself, and he sees every single factor that plays into your life. He will not leave you destitute. He is an attentive and caring provider, and you will rejoice when you experience how he meets your needs and exceeds your expectations! You can count on him; he will not fail you.

Provider, I choose again to trust your faithful character. You are rich in love and mercy, and you have not let me waste away yet. I will trust you to come through for me where I have run out of my own solutions. You are wiser than I am; work it all out and fill me with peace so I may rest in you.

Reason for Joy

Don't be sad, because the joy of the Lord
will make you strong.
NEHEMIAH 8:10 NCV

Sorrow goes hand-in-hand with loss. There is no shortcut to healing the depth of grief; it must be walked through, embraced, and experienced. It is not something anyone wishes, but it is still a part of life. If we give ourselves to it, we will find our hearts expand in every way: to experience greater depths of joy, awe, and gratitude, as well as the pain that leads us there.

The joy of the Lord is our strength in every season. When we have run out of reasons to be happy, God reveals that his joy is not dependent on our changing moods. It is like a rushing river, flowing through the landscapes of our hearts, bringing life to all it touches. There is no striving in it; we simply need to let its waters flow over us and we will feel the relief and strength it offers.

Wonderful Lord, teach me what it is to be strong in your joy. I know that it does not ignore realities or pain; show me what it's like to dwell in your peace and joy while I walk through the suffering of this season.

Scope of Life

His mercy is for those who fear him
from generation to generation.
LUKE 1:50 NRSV

Our life's scope is so much greater and more meaningful when we realize that the power of it does not begin or end with us or with this current generation. Are we building a life for ourselves: our own comfort, ease, and prosperity? Or are we looking with a broader lens? How does what we build in this life affect the coming generations?

God's mercy is the same in abundance throughout every historical age. It is not greater in its power now than it was in the time of Moses. It will be as full of God's unending love when our grandchildren's children are in the prime of their lives as it is this very moment. May we live with intention, planting the seeds of his mercy and justice for future generations to feast upon.

God of mercy, I want to live with intention and purpose that goes beyond my small existence. I want to partner with your heart of love that considers others above myself. Teach me to walk in your ways, sowing love and mercy with every decision I make. Take my meager offerings and make them grow in your kindness.

Rest in the Embrace

If I say, "My foot slips,"
Your mercy, O LORD, will hold me up.
PSALM 94:18 NKJV

There is not a misstep we could make where God's strong arm of mercy wouldn't reach out and steady us. He is the support of our very lives: the foundation of faithful love that holds us up in every season. We cannot fall outside of his grip of grace. If we were to dive off the cliff of despair, even then we could not escape his loyal love that catches us.

Take heart today. God is your guard, your support, and your defense. You are not lost. You are not broken. You are not alone. Rest in the embrace of your God and find the comfort that is closer than your suffering. You are held by love.

Mighty God, you are my hope and my strength. I have nothing without your love. I am depleted, but you are abundant in mercy, and you never let me go. Fill me afresh today with the peace of your presence and hold me together with your tender love.

State of Grief

I am weary with my sighing;
Every night I make my bed swim,
I dissolve my couch with my tears.
My eye has wasted away with grief;
It has become old because of all my adversaries.

PSALM 6:6-8 NASB

Have you grown tired of fighting the sorrow you feel? Have you been swimming in tears from sundown to sunup? Whatever the state of your grief, know that your God sees you and meets you in it. There is no amount of mourning that can drive him away. He rushes into the suffering with you. His comfort is so very near.

Don't hold back from him today. He can handle the breadth and depth of your raw emotion. The Comforter wraps around you with love and mercy that sees and understands. What he offers, no one else can. He gives relief for your weariness. He is with you now; will you listen for his words of tenderness?

God, I am so tired of feeling such exhausting sorrow. I can't escape it, and I need to know you in the middle of this dark night. Show me your face and speak so I can hear you. I must know you. Reveal yourself to me.

The Same Love

If there is any encouragement in Christ, any comfort from love,
any participation in the Spirit, any affection and sympathy,
complete my joy by being of the same mind, having the same love,
being in full accord and of one mind.

PHILIPPIANS 2:1-2 ESV

We are all called to the same love though it takes on many different expressions. Where there is mercy, there is God in our midst. The spirit of generosity reflects the kingdom of heaven. Compassion is a manifestation of God in us. So, let us offer each other what God offers us: the comfort of love without thought for what we can gain, and the kindness of believing in each other's goodness.

Where there is loyal love, there is unity. May we be unified in the same generous mercy that we receive in unending measure from the heart of our good Father. There is no better time than now to take up his ways and leave our own self-seeking ones behind.

Holy One, you are the perfect picture of unity. Father, Son, and Spirit, all distinct and yet dwelling in the same nature. I want to be like you in love, reflecting your generosity in my life. May I give as freely as I receive, for you are rich in mercy.

Full of Questions

If you are truly wise, you'll learn from what I've told you.
It's time for you to consider these profound lessons
of God's great love and mercy.

PSALM 107:43 TPT

Today, let your attention turn to the Lord in his nearness. His presence surrounds you with peace, clarity, and comfort. Where there is angst, lay it at the feet of Jesus and ask for his perfect perspective. Where there is disappointment, offer it up with an invitation for God's gift of gracious redemption.

It is wise to press into the heart of God when you are full of questions. Why not let him speak into them? He is full of wisdom and understanding, giving revelations of his kindness freely to those who look to him. So, beloved, look to him today.

Wise God, I look to you today. Meet me right where I am in this moment and bring light and life as I offer you the questions of my heart. Give insight where I have none. Teach me in your wisdom to see things the way you do. Your love and mercy are ever expanding, so may my heart also expand with the revelations you give in accordance with your Word of truth.

Ability to Persevere

*Keep yourselves in the love of God,
waiting for the mercy of our Lord Jesus Christ
that leads to eternal life.*

JUDE 1:21 ESV

When you have run out of your own resources of love and understanding, know that there is always more flowing from the heart of the Father. Be continually filled up with his mercy as often as you can. There's no need to ever run dry. But when you do, there is a fountain flowing over your life where you can be refreshed and restored.

Come and drink from the fountain of God's love today. It will remove the dust of disappointment and refresh your resolve to stay clothed in the cloak of his kindness. It is the source of your strength, giving you the ability to persevere. Keep going, for you have not reached the end of his loyal love.

Jesus, I need a fresh reminder of your present love in my life. Pour out your Spirit that brings life to barren places. I need you; I depend on you. You are the only thing that keeps me going.

Refreshed in Clarity

You will increase my honor,
and comfort me once again.
PSALM 71:21 NRSV

Have you reached the end of your rope? Are you at a loss for what to do whether it be with family, work, or even your own healing? There is one who never grows weary and who never loses sight of the big picture. Run into the safety of God's presence today and find yourself refreshed in the clarity and peace he holds.

God is your ultimate advocate always working on your behalf. He does not let anything in your life go to waste; rather, he brings redemption to every part, weaving his mercy faithfully through your story. He gives you honor for the ashes in your life. He trades his joy for your mourning. He is working, and everything he does is marked by his faithful love. You will see it, and you will revel in his goodness once again.

Faithful Father, all of my life is in your hands. I cannot make treasure out of the ruins of my life, but I know that you will unearth and show me what you have been doing even in my darkest hours. You make all things new—even me. Don't stop, Lord.

Not Sick of You

The Lord wants to show his mercy to you.
He wants to rise and comfort you.
The Lord is a fair God,
and everyone who waits for his help will be happy.
ISAIAH 30:18 NCV

God's ways are so much purer than our own. He does not grow weary in kindness, nor does he worry for you. He sees everything clearly, and he's got a handle on your life. He sees what you cannot, and he works all things together for your good. Will you let him rise and comfort you today?

Even when you're sick of yourself, God is not tired of you. He longs to wrap you up in the comfort of his compassion and restore your hope as you rest in him. Lean back into his everlasting mercy; there is more than enough to surround you. Wait on his help, for he will not fail you. Let him take the lead today, and you will not be disheartened.

Lord, you are so extravagant in love; I can't comprehend the fullness of it. I give up keeping you at a distance. You're the only one who can breathe life into my soul. Revive me in your presence and restore me in your comfort.

Hungry Heart

The Sovereign LORD has given me his words of wisdom,
so that I know how to comfort the weary.
Morning by morning he wakens me
and opens my understanding to his will.

ISAIAH 50:4 NLT

Every day is a new opportunity to lean into learning the ways of our good Father. There is more wisdom, more revelation, more understanding to be found in him. The Spirit is our guide and our teacher. He is our holy help and the epitome of wisdom. He is everything we need and more.

Is your heart hungry? Feast on the Word that he offers you. There is not a shortage of knowledge and insight in him. He will give you the understanding that you crave. The more you consume his love and open your heart to his ways, the greater capacity you will have to know him in deeper ways.

Sovereign Lord, you are the way, the truth, and the life. I come to you, seeking more knowledge of your ways. I want to walk in the light of your wisdom and revelation every day. I want to know you in deeper ways than I ever have before. Meet me, guide me, and lead me further into your love.

Allowed to Feel

"Now is your time of grief,
but I will see you again and you will rejoice,
and no one will take away your joy."
JOHN 16:22 NIV

In the pangs of deep sorrow, when the memory of lighter days does nothing to console your grief, the Lord your God keeps you company with the comfort of his presence. This will not last forever: the weeping and mourning. But don't try to rush through it. Let yourself feel the depths of the loss and invite the Holy Spirit into it.

You will rejoice again, but if you are in the depths of sorrow, today is not that day. And that's okay! Feel it, whatever it is, and let it lead you to the rivers of living water flowing inside of you where spirit communes with Spirit. There is no hurry here. Take every moment as it comes and know that you will taste the joy of brighter and lighter days again.

Light of the world, you are the one I look to now. I am done trying to fight the tide of my grief. I know that you will not let it wash me away from your presence; I could never escape you! Even so, Lord, meet me in the middle of it. I need you; breathe your breath of life into me and comfort my broken heart.

Hold Me

Sing for joy, O heavens, and exult, O earth;
break forth, O mountains, into singing!
For the LORD has comforted his people,
and will have compassion on his suffering one.
ISAIAH 49:13 NRSV

Everything the Lord does, he does with compassion. There are no ulterior motives hidden in his heart; he is always rich in mercy and abundant in pure love. He does not leave you; no, he never abandons his people. He is close in comfort. Have you felt the touch of his tender presence today?

When you suffer, the Lord pours love over your anguish. He will not let your heart shatter; he binds up the brokenhearted and makes them whole in his wonderful kindness. He will do this for you. When you find yourself unable to go on in your own strength, he rushes to you, gathers you nearer and carries you through the darkest night. He holds you, so don't be afraid.

Comforter, I need your arms to hold me up, for I am falling apart! Let your love wash over me and heal every broken part. When I don't know how to pray or what to say, come close and do what only you can do.

Beautiful Fruit

The name of the Lord is blessed and lifted high!
For his marvelous miracle of mercy protected me
when I was overwhelmed by my enemies.
PSALM 31:21 TPT

God's reputation as defender of the helpless is not something to overlook. When we cannot see a way out of the battles of this life and it looks as if the enemy will take us out with the sheer force of opposition, there is a help that is stronger rising up on our behalf.

The Lord works his miracles of mercy in and through our lives over and over again—more than we can recognize. Don't lose heart and don't give up hope today. God's faithful fingerprints are all over your life. When you come out of this deep valley, and you look back to the path you tread, you will see a garden of beautiful fruit bursting at the seams. You are not alone. Trust him today.

Protector, rise up on my behalf and save me. I have no strength, and I've run out of any will to try and strategize my way out of this. You know best; don't leave me to be overtaken by fear. Show yourself, my God and my rescue.

Due Date

For every matter there is a time and judgment,
Though the misery of man increases greatly.
ECCLESIASTES 8:6 NKJV

Has your timeline passed its due date of when you thought you would feel better? Perhaps you've thrown it out altogether, realizing your life will never be the same as it was. There is nothing wrong with changing your mind or expanding the possibilities of life with your growing understanding.

It's not wrong for us to set expectations, but we must be gentle with ourselves when we realize that we cannot control the outcome. We never could. God's wisdom takes into account all that we cannot see or comprehend, as well as all that we do. His timing is perfect; he will neither be late or early. Do we trust him in the waiting?

Perfect One, I recognize that I am limited in understanding. I don't want to keep a tight fist, grasping whatever it is that I think I can control when you are right here asking me to trust you with my heart and my hopes. As I look to you, remind me of your faithful and loving nature that will not lead me into despair but into freedom.

Reach of Plans

"I know that You can do all things,
And that no purpose of Yours can be thwarted."

JOB 42:2 NASB

God's plans are not like ours that only take so much into account. We may consider our comfort, our goals, and our loved ones, but how far does the reach of our plans actually go? The wise and compassionate Lord sees what we do not and plans accordingly. And he is good!

The same one who promised it will fulfill it in his faithfulness. He knows how to turn our mourning to dancing, and he also knows the time to do it. We can rest in his goodness, knowing that he will do all that he set out to do. And everything he does is with mercy and love as his signature. He will surprise us with his thoughtfulness.

God, you are the one who put breath inside my lungs and caused my heart to start beating in my mother's womb. You have not missed a single detail of my life or anyone else's, and you're not about to change now. I trust you with my life. Rain your goodness down on me once again, that I may marvel at your compassion!

At Every Juncture

"Can a woman forget the baby she nurses?
Can she feel no kindness for the child to which she gave birth?
Even if she could forget her children, I will not forget you."
ISAIAH 49:15 NCV

Like a loving and devoted parent, God cares for us. Even better than the most attentive father, he sees and meets our needs. More consistent than a faithful mother, he teaches and comforts us. He is full of affection toward us. Does it seem too good to be true? Oh, but it is!

He is more thoughtful than a devoted friend, more committed than a loyal lover, and kinder than the most jovial grandparent. He is better than we expect him to be at every juncture. Just you wait, he will prove it again to you. He will never forget you, not in your triumphs or your letdowns. He is close, and he is working on your behalf.

Lord, I want to know your goodness. I need to know you more. I want to fellowship with your Spirit and know your thoughts toward me. Speak; I am listening.

Light of Discernment

The wise see danger ahead and avoid it,
but fools keep going and get into trouble.

PROVERBS 27:12 NCV

As children of the Most High, we are privileged with access to God's unending truth through his mercy. The Spirit of wisdom and insight dwells within us. Where we fall short in knowledge, God is full of wisdom for every problem we face. We are not beggars, waiting for scraps of revelation to fall our way.

May we press into the abundance of God's heart where we find the understanding of his great love that includes everything we do not know to take into consideration. When we align our thoughts and hearts with God's truth and unchanging character, we have the discernment we need to make wise choices. We are not helpless in decisions; we have the light of life as our counselor and guide!

Wise God, I lean into your heart of love that fills me with the peace of your presence. This peace brings clarity to the thoughts of my mind and the feelings of my heart; I will not waver in wisdom with your faithful voice instructing me.

Around the Mountain

Let us stop going over the basic teachings about Christ again and again. Let us go on instead and become mature in our understanding. Surely we don't need to start again with the fundamental importance of repenting from evil deeds and placing our faith in God.

HEBREWS 6:1 NLT

How many times have you found yourself back at the beginning? Whether it's in life, love, or faith, you may think that it's all linear: like a line running from the start to the end. But the cycles of life show us that we tread a path that's much more like going around a mountain; we circle around, but we find ourselves higher with each lap.

Do not be discouraged if you feel like you've circled around to a place you thought you had left behind. If you look closely, you will notice that everything is not the same as it was before. You have higher perspective. Let the Lord show you what it is you have to learn from this new place that somehow feels familiar. You don't need to question your salvation again. Each time you find yourself in a well-known place, find the pieces that you missed before. You are not falling backward; you are circling higher.

Faithful One, when I hear the old stories of unworthiness and shame calling out to me, I will remember that they are not my portion. Give me your perspective to see that there is more to where I'm at right now than where I've been before. I trust you; I'm ready for your better word.

A Valuable Trait

You need to persevere so that when you have done the will of God,
you will receive what he has promised.
HEBREWS 10:36 NIV

Don't give up. You have not reached the end of God's faithfulness in your life. His mercy has not suddenly run out, and his restoration work has not halted. He is working in the details of your story, and he is weaving it all together with the strong cord of his love. If you struggle to see what he is doing, ask him today for eyes to see.

Perseverance is not some useless coping tool. It is a valuable trait to hold onto. Have you determined that God's ways are better than your own? If not, look again at his uncompromising nature. He is trustworthy. Keep going in love, and don't give up hope. He is leading you still, and he is forever good.

God, give me the strength to persist in hope no matter what my circumstances look like. I don't want to be unsure of your love; fill me with the overwhelming goodness of your presence today so I remember the hope I am holding onto.

Unchangeable

*Don't set the affections of your heart on this world
or in loving the things of the world.
The love of the Father and the love of the world are incompatible.*

1 JOHN 2:15 TPT

When our love for the things of this world outweighs the love we have for God, we will never find satisfaction. This world, along with everything in it, will pass away. We cannot control when or how our lives will change, though we try. Of all that we can influence, there is so much more that we have no power over.

Instead of fixating on the changeable things of this life, why don't we set our eyes on that which will never be taken away? Our good Father is always working on our behalf, and his love is like a rushing river, sweeping over us all the days of our lives. Let's fix our eyes on the unseen eternal, where mercy and love dwell in unending measure. We will not always see dimly through a dark glass. The day is coming when God will be revealed in all of his glory, and we won't be able to help the awe and love we feel.

Lord, I choose to set my mind and heart on you today. You are so much better than anything I could find to temporarily satisfy me in this life. Your love outlasts the sun, moon, and stars. I know that your love will change me, and I want to be consumed by it here and now.

Swept to Sea

Create in me a clean heart, O God,
and put a new and right spirit within me.
PSALM 51:10 NRSV

Today is a day of restoration. It is an opportunity for being made whole. This is the moment you have been waiting for—the chance to be made new in the refreshing living waters of God's presence. There is nothing that can separate you from the tidal wave of his love. Let it wash over you, sweeping you into the sea of his great joy and peace.

God is full of glory light that shines in even the darkest nights. You are caught in his light. Do not try to hide from him; he longs to restore you today in his unwavering mercy. If you let it, it will revive you. Don't ruminate on yesterday or worry about tomorrow; here is God with the fullness of his love. Your present moment is saturated with his kindness.

God, cleanse me in the living water of your love today. Wash over me and refresh every weary part of my heart. Soak into the soil of my soul and bring life where there has been drought.

The Source

All things are of God, who has reconciled us to Himself
through Jesus Christ, and has given us the ministry of reconciliation.
2 CORINTHIANS 5:18 NKJV

There is not a joy or a delight in this world that does not find
its roots in the source of life—God. He has reconciled us to him
through the resurrection of Jesus. His power, at work in our lives,
breaks the chains of death and despair. Where there are glimmers
of light, we can be sure that there is God too.

Let everything we do be fueled by the great mercy and love of
our God and King. Our very lives, built upon the foundation of his
faithfulness, are reflections of his kindness and restorative nature.
He has not finished with us yet, and he won't stop moving in love
toward us.

Jesus, you are the bridge that leads me straight to the heart of
the Father. I will not build my life on anything but you. I know
that you are a firm foundation. All the goodness I seek is found in
you, and all the goodness I find in life is a gift from your hand.

Temporary Returns

"Don't work for the food that spoils. Work for the food that stays good always and gives eternal life. The Son of Man will give you this food, because on him God the Father has put his power."

JOHN 6:27 NCV

When we set our minds on God's kingdom and ways, our thoughts will be transformed by the hope of glory to come. There is a reward that is better than any we could find in temporary labors and returns. Let's set our lives according to the rhythm of the faithful love that leads us. There is fruit that will last in following God's better ways.

What have you been pouring your energy into lately? What tracks does your mind follow? If you are exhausted of worry, tired of never having enough resources, and realize that you have been striving instead of resting in the confidence of God's provision, today is a fresh opportunity for you to refocus. Spend some time soaking in God's Word, letting his voice refresh and restore your soul today.

Jesus, I look to you again today. I have been so distracted by the demands of life that anxiety has led me away from your rest instead of into your heart of peace. Refill and refresh me today with your Word.

More Wisdom

How blessed is the man who finds wisdom
And the man who gains understanding.

PROVERBS 3:13 NASB

No matter how much time we spend reading, learning, and practicing the knowledge of God, there is always more wisdom to be found in him. He did not simply prescribe us a set of rules to follow and then guarantee holiness; he made a way for living relationship that transforms us by its depths.

Wisdom is found in the person of God. When was the last time you sought God's perspective on a matter that had you stumped? He wants you to press into him; he has so much to share with you. There is a wealth of wisdom in the Word of God, and there is revelation to be found in his presence. He will not be silent. Ask, and he will answer.

Wise God, I want to know you more. I don't want to just know about you, I want to know the tender tone of your voice and the ways that you speak to me. I am listening.

Familiar with Suffering

Going a little farther, he fell on the ground and prayed that,
if it were possible, the hour might pass from him.
And he said, "Abba, Father, all things are possible for you.
Remove this cup from me. Yet not what I will, but what you will."
MARK 14:35–36 ESV

Jesus, the Son of God, was not without trouble in this world. He was not without sorrow, agony, and suffering. He is acquainted with our suffering; he knows just what we are going through because he has also gone through it. Find rest and comfort in the humanity of Jesus today. He knows how you feel.

Will you also follow the example of Jesus' surrender to the Father? Even though he didn't want to walk into pain and suffering, he knew that it was coming. Instead of resisting it, he submitted to the Father's will. Are you resisting God's comfort in the midst of your pain? Are you trying to keep yourself from feeling the weight of your suffering? Follow Jesus' lead and see where it takes you today.

Son of Man, I had forgotten that you are familiar with my suffering. You know what it feels like to be staring down immeasurable pain. You grieved and struggled, and yet you still submitted to the Father. Teach me to do the same.

Supernaturally Infused

I have saved these most important truths for last:
Be supernaturally infused with strength
through your life-union with the Lord Jesus.
Stand victorious with the force of his explosive power
flowing in and through you.

EPHESIANS 6:10 TPT

There is gloriously good news to be found in Jesus' life, death, and resurrection. Though he was a man, accustomed to the humanity of this life, he was also God. The power that broke death's finality and resurrected him from the grave is the same power living in us through God's Spirit.

There is so much more available to us in the present moment than we can imagine. There is victory in the Spirit of Jesus, who is our ever-present companion and help. His strength is our strength, and it is not feeble. There is unhindered connection and power in him, and it is ours today.

Savior, you are the overcoming one—the one who defeated the power of sin and death. You are my strong and mighty tower. You are the one I rely on, the one I need, and you're right here. Fill me with your victorious strength today.

Direction Challenge

Whether you turn to the right or to the left,
your ears will hear a voice behind you, saying,
"This is the way; walk in it."
ISAIAH 30:21 NIV

Are you confused by the direction you should be going? Are you unsure where to focus your energy? Are you questioning whether you're in the right place? Whatever your questions, God is full of wisdom for you. He will be your faithful guide as you venture through every difficulty. He will lead you as you consider each possibility.

Tune your ear to his voice today. He is always speaking. Look at the evidence of his love and faithfulness in your life. Align your mind with the fruit of his peace that passes understanding. He will guide you with the clarity of his understanding. Trust him; he knows what he is doing.

Faithful One, I want to follow your leading in every area of my life. I know that you see what I cannot: the bigger picture as well as every detail. Lead me in love, and I will follow!

At Home

"Those who love me will keep my word, and my Father will love them,
and we will come to them and make our home with them."
JOHN 14:23 NRSV

What a wonderful mystery that the King of kings makes his home in us. His Spirit was poured out onto the disciples on the day of Pentecost, and it is the same Spirit who dwells in us. What a wonder! Is there any better hope than the gift of God's presence with us?

He who has made his home in us is also the one in whom we find our true home. We find all belonging and acceptance as his children. We are not made to be blind followers of a demanding rule-giver; rather, we have been adopted into a family of those who find their true selves fully embraced in the delight of a good Father.

Father, you are the giver of all good things, and the best gift you have given is yourself! I am undone at the reality of the fullness of your kind nature pouring out over my life at all times. Why would I turn away from such a wonderful Father? I'm running into your goodness again. Your kindness soothes my soul.

Powerful Intention

The plans of the diligent lead surely to plenty,
But those of everyone who is hasty, surely to poverty.
PROVERBS 21:5 NKJV

There is tremendous honor to be found in the faithful follow-through of God's people. God is eternally consistent, always doing what he said he would do. He's not looking for perfection from us, but we should consider what we give our yeses to as well as when to say no.

Do we rush to meet needs without considering if it's something that will require more than we are able to offer in the long run? There's nothing wrong with short-term commitments, but we should not blindly run into different pursuits with zero foresight. Intention is powerful as well as consistency. Above all, may we be both deliberate and reliable in love.

God over all, I know that you see everything clearly—the past, present, and future. Help me to align my heart, values, and plans with your faithful love. Give me the discernment I need when making commitments, so I diligently follow through with honor.

Great Architect

It is by faith we understand that the whole world was made by God's command so what we see was made by something that cannot be seen.
HEBREWS 11:3 NCV

God is the great architect of all we see, know, and understand; he is also the creator of all that we can't see, have yet to learn, and don't comprehend. Everything finds its source and its fulfillment in him. We are no different. When we look to his perspective and seek his wisdom, we will find revelation that broadens our limited worldviews.

By faith, we understand that God is the masterful artist behind the workings of the universe. Everything he does oozes creativity. We are images of a creative mastermind. When was the last time you considered the miracle of you? You are a unique reflection of the beauty of the Maker, and there is no one else like you! Look into his glory today, and ask for eyes to see yourself in him and him in you.

Creator, I want to see what you see when you look at me. I know that I am not a mistake, and the way you made me was with intention and delight. May I come alive in your affection today, knowing that I am fully embraced by, and belong to, you.

September

"Keep watch and pray,
so that you will not give in to temptation.
For the spirit is willing,
but the body is weak!"

MATTHEW 26:41 NLT

Reflection of Compassion

The Lord is not slow about His promise, as some count slowness,
but is patient toward you, not wishing for any to perish
but for all to come to repentance.

2 PETER 3:9 NASB

When was the last time you considered God's timing a reflection
of his innate compassion? There is nothing about him that does
not include his magnanimous mercy. If you have grown tired of
waiting on God's answers, press into his heart and ask him for his
perspective. He will not turn you away.

If you can see everything God does through the lens of his love,
your heart will grow in confidence and trust as you wait on him. He
will not fail to come through for you. Here, in the in-between, don't
pull away from him. You have his attention; will you give him yours?

Merciful Father, how quick I am to pull back when I feel as
if I can't understand you. Today, I'm doing the opposite; I'm
pressing into you. Speak to me and show me what it is that
you are doing. Remind me of your great grace and patience.
I need a revelation of your goodness again.

Hope Revived

"You gave me life and showed me kindness,
and in your providence watched over my spirit."
JOB 10:12 NIV

There is not a moment of your life where God, rich in kindness, is not present. He is here with the comfort you long for and the encouragement your heart needs. He does not force himself on you; rather, he patiently and gently watches over you. When you are ready to invite him nearer, he reveals how very close he has been all along.

Will you invite him to show you his wonderful ways today? He is not demanding; he knows just what you need. Ask him for a fresh revelation of his present goodness, and he will revive your hope. Your Father cares deeply for you, and he is working all things in your life to come together with his mercy. Like an artist masterfully weaves different threads together into a beautiful tapestry, so he is weaving every part of your life together with his wonderful love.

Life Giver, I long for a fresh revelation of your kindness today. Open my eyes to see what you're doing right now in my life. I invite your perspective.

Standing on Love

Let us be thankful, because we have a kingdom that cannot be shaken.
We should worship God in a way that pleases him with respect and fear.
HEBREWS 12:28 NCV

The kingdom of God is an unshakable fortress. With strong mercy as its foundation, it holds up to the weight of God's glory. Where do you see the evidence of God's remarkable love that has lasted through the storms and quakes of life? His peace is the atmosphere of his presence; have you breathed it in lately?

Whatever it is that you're facing today, know that God's ways are unchanging. He is quick to offer compassion and slow to anger. He is patient and kind. He is strong and a righteous judge. He is not weak; you can stand upon his love and know that it will never leave you. You are his. How does your heart respond to this truth today?

Mighty God, remind me of your power at work in the world. You are the God who created everything—including me. May I not forget that your kindness is not a character weakness but a tremendous strength that I can build my life upon. You are so worthy of all my trust.

Get Real

Whoever conceals his transgressions will not prosper,
but he who confesses and forsakes them will obtain mercy.
PROVERBS 28:13 ESV

Have you gotten real with yourself and with God lately? It is good to consider where you are in this moment. What are you feeling? Get curious about the emotions, or even the lack of them, today. There is no right or wrong feeling—just the honesty of what it is. His wisdom will lead you in how to surrender it to him.

There is no shame in God's love, and his love permeates every cell with his presence. You are encompassed by love, for the Spirit of the Lord is upon you. There is greater freedom for you in his mercy. Let him meet you with his generous compassion in your great need. He is able, and more than willing to love you to life whenever you ask.

Gracious God, here I am heart laid bare before you today. I don't want to hide from you any longer. I long for restoration; will you give it today? I trust your refreshing love to wash over me as I loosen my hold on what no longer serves me well.

Incomparably Pure

Your laws are my treasure;
they are my heart's delight.
PSALM 119:111 NLT

The ways of God are a marvelous mystery; how could one so perfect exist? How could he love without end no matter what we have done? His incomparably pure nature confounds the mind. When we spend time not just getting to know *about* him but getting to know him through fellowship with his Spirit, we grow in wisdom.

When we know what God is like, his telltale kindness through however many chances he gives, keeping no record of wrongs, how could we not love him? When we know the tone of his tender voice, how could we not be soothed by his words? He is so much better than we've been told, and it is our delight to discover this over and over again.

Holy One, you are wonderful. There is no one else like you. As you continue to reveal your goodness in my life, may it fill my heart with wonder. I am in awe of how rich the treasure of your presence is.

Endless Sea of Love

*"Show mercy and compassion for others,
just as your heavenly Father overflows with mercy
and compassion for all."*
LUKE 6:36 TPT

God's heart of love is wider than the vast skies, deeper than the oceans' depths, and longer than the memory of mankind. It is like a fountain, always flowing with the pure waters of his mercy. There is healing in his affection. It restores what was broken whether it be our relationships or our hearts.

He is abounding in loyal kindness. Do our lives overflow with the generosity of his compassion? Every moment is an opportunity to pour out what has been poured into us. Love will never run dry when its source is the endless sea of God's very nature.

Compassionate One, I am so thankful for your love that washes over me, fills me up, and flows out from my life. Increase my capacity for mercy as I practice giving it away just as you do. Your ways are better than my own, so I will follow your lead.

Love Never Fails

*"Do to others what you want them to do to you.
This is the meaning of the law of Moses
and the teaching of the prophets."*

MATTHEW 7:12 NCV

There is honor in loving God and pouring out our hearts to him. But our lives show the utmost devotion to him when we follow his law of love: to treat others with the honor and respect we long for. Kindness is not a weak virtue; it honors others' lives as our own. The golden rule still encompasses the whole of the law of the prophets as Jesus told his disciples.

Loving others is no small task. It keeps no record of wrongs, it is consistently kind to all, it is not jealous when others succeed, and it does not boast or brag. It does not shame others, and it does not seek to boost oneself over another. It believes the best for others, and it never gives up. Love, as 1 Corinthians 13 says, never fails.

Father of love, thank you for the reminder of what your love looks like. Clothe my mind and heart in your compassion that makes no excuses for offense.

Certainly Heard

Certainly God has heard me;
He has attended to the voice of my prayer.
PSALM 66:19 NKJV

God has no limits on his capacity in any way. Where we are confined to the bounds of our understanding, God is not. He is able to see every detail and not lose sight of a single one no matter how small. He is able to account for the hairs on our heads; how much more does he listen to our cries?

Your prayer does not go unnoticed. He hears you, even when the words never pass your lips. He knows you, and he cares for you. He is such an attentive and kindhearted Father. He will not disappoint you; he won't ignore your pleas. He has heard it all, and he will come through for you. Just you wait and see.

Faithful God, answer me today. My heart is encouraged in the confidence of you hearing my prayers. But Lord, take it a step further. Attend to me, speak to me, answer me!

Deep Springs

"Because of your father's God, who helps you, because of the Almighty, who blesses you with blessings of the skies above, blessings of the deep springs below, blessings of the breast and womb."

GENESIS 49:25 NIV

There is encouragement to be found in the histories of those who have walked with God before us. The testimony of a life that has seen God's faithfulness show up time and again is powerful. It is full of fruit that we can take, eat, and be nourished by. It is encouragement to our hearts especially when we walk the unknown paths that require radical courage and trust in the Lord.

Today, look for the testimony of those who have walked through dark nights and come through on the other side with God's joy and peace still covering them. Listen to stories of those who have hit rock bottom in this life and still proclaim the goodness of God. They speak of the deep wells of God's faithful love. Drink deeply today.

Holy Spirit, lead me to the testimonies of your people that will encourage me where I am today. I know I am not alone in walking through the disorientation of loss; there are those who have gone before me. Encourage me through the lives of others who did not give up. Help me to be like them.

A Firm Rock

"You will have confidence, because there is hope;
you will be protected and take your rest in safety."
JOB 11:18 NRSV

When grief shakes the walls of your life causing some to come crashing down, are you able to see what is left? Not everything has been destroyed, though it is right to mourn what is forever changed. Do not despair today; do you see that the foundation beneath you is a firm rock?

All hope is not lost today. Can you spot the fingerprints of mercy within your life still? God has not left you to rebuild a life for yourself. He is the master restorer, and he will do what you could only dream of. Rest in the confidence of your faithful God, who works on your behalf. He is both skilled and trustworthy. Let your expectations align with his character.

My God, thank you for being a firm foundation that holds up my life. Come closer as I turn my attention to you. I long for your refreshing presence to revive my weary heart in hope again.

Forever Good

*Jesus Christ is the same
yesterday and today and forever.*
HEBREWS 13:8 NASB

Every new day brings with it new opportunities as well as new challenges. Change is guaranteed in this life; we cannot avoid it. Jesus is the only unchangeable one who remains the same throughout the ages. His love is pure, his mercy overflowing, and his justice immoveable.

When we're looking for encouragement, where do we turn? Do we look for clues for better things to come in the world around us? If we will persevere, there is always more hope than we can sense in the moment. Let us fix our eyes on Jesus, the origin and the culmination of our faith. He is forever good!

Jesus Christ, you are the one I look to in the shifting winds of the storms of life. I look to you on the sunny days and on the cloudy ones. I look to you today. Reveal your unmistakable, glorious goodness to me again. I depend on your unrelenting love to steady me.

Courage of Love

Remember to stay alert and hold firmly to all that you believe.
Be mighty and full of courage.
1 CORINTHIANS 16:13 TPT

When we are tempted to give up all hope, there is one who never lets go. Will we turn our attention to the grip of grace that holds our lives steady? God has not changed in mercy toward us. His kindness still covers us completely. His loyal love is doing the work of restoration already, perhaps in ways that we cannot see clearly yet.

Let us not grow weary in trust today. God's heart is a safe place to remain. Let's not let the winds of worry convince us that God has changed. His intentions remain steadfast and true. Let us connect our lives to the vine of his mercy, aligning ourselves in his love once again. He is with us both now and forevermore.

Lord, strengthen my heart in the courage of your bold love today. I feel the temptation to worry and let anxiety take over the peace I have in you. I will not give up hope today, for you are unchanging in your remarkable love.

A Shared Load

Confess your sins to each other and pray for each other so that you may be healed. The earnest prayer of a righteous person has great power and produces wonderful results.

JAMES 5:16 NLT

When is the last time you shared your struggles with someone you trust? We are not meant to wrestle through weighty things alone. God has set you in community, in family. Think of someone who is reliable and trustworthy and consider sharing with them what you are experiencing in this current season. A shared load is lighter.

There is no need to go it alone whatever it is that you are going through. You have God, and he is the most reliable advocate and friend, but you also have others. There is solace to be found. The prayers of others hold you up in ways that encourage and strengthen you. What if instead of keeping your heart isolated in pain, you chose to lean on a trusted friend?

Lord, help me to be courageous in vulnerability today. As I share my struggles, will you lighten the load of my loneliness? Bring to mind who I can lean on in this time. I know you won't let me down.

Endless Delight

You make known to me the path of life;
in your presence there is fullness of joy;
at your right hand are pleasures forevermore.
PSALM 16:11 ESV

In the presence of God, there is fullness of joy. He does not force his happiness on us, giving us a list of reasons why we shouldn't feel sorrow. That's not how he works. Joy is deeper than contentment; it is a river that brings life even in the driest drought. There are endless delights and pleasures in the kingdom of our God, and he gladly shares them with us. They are not consolation prizes; rather, they are evidence of his glorious goodness that never lets up or lets go.

Even in the valley of the shadow of death, there are treasures to be found. God does not walk with us and leave his love behind; it meets us wherever we are. Today, as we look to God, may we see the evidence of his mercy, encountering us with the reality of the fullness of his affection.

Giver of life, flow into every part of my day, into every detail. I long to see the mark of your presence in my life; encourage me in your joy and reveal the glory of your kindness that always overflows from your heart to mine.

When I Am Weak

For Christ's sake, I delight in weaknesses, in insults, in hardships, in persecutions, in difficulties. For when I am weak, then I am strong.
2 CORINTHIANS 12:10 NIV

When we are weak, it is not a sign of our failure in faith. When we are bombarded by hardship, it does not mean that we have veered off the path of God's plan for our lives. When we are mocked and misunderstood, it is not evidence that we have messed up. No, all these things and more are a part of the human experience.

There is no reason to despair in faith when we struggle in life. Paul said that he was able to find joy for Christ's sake in the trials. When we learn to do the same, inviting the Spirit of God to teach us to suffer with Christ and not on our own, we find that nothing can stop the love of God from growing, filling, and strengthening us. When we are weak, there is an invitation to know Christ's overpowering strength.

Lord, I see now that my struggle does not mean that I have somehow failed you. Empower me with your Spirit that I may learn to walk in the strength of your glorious grace. When my pride is hit, what a wonderful opportunity to humbly walk with you.

In the Meantime

It is not yet time for the message to come true,
but that time is coming soon; the message will come true.
It may seem like a long time, but be patient and wait for it,
because it will surely come; it will not be delayed.

HABAKKUK 3:2 NCV

While you're waiting on the fulfillment of God's promises in your life, how does your heart respond? God is trustworthy; he is faithful. He's not a devious man that he would lure us with false promises. He is loyal in love, and he will do what he said.

In the meantime, there is so much hope to be found. There is abundance of joy in his presence. There is peace that keeps our hearts and minds calm in the truth of his unchanging goodness. When our timelines have come and gone and been made completely obsolete, God is undeterred in his plans. He has not forgotten a single detail. Rest in his faithfulness today, for he has not lost sight of you.

Holy God, you see the end from the beginning and everything between. I am so limited in my scope of understanding; when I grow frustrated at your timing, reassure my heart with hope. Give me eyes to see you. You are so much bigger and better than I can comprehend.

Promoting Peace

*Let us pursue the things which make for peace
and the things by which one may edify another.*
ROMANS 14:19 NKJV

In these tumultuous times what are we giving our attention and emotional energy to? Are we promoters of peace that seek truth and understanding not to silence another's point of view? When our views are challenged, do we quickly jump to the defense of our values, dismissing the person in front of us?

Pursuing peace means that we pursue God's view of our situations. He who is patient and kind is our ultimate example. He does not deal in shame or disrespect, not even toward those who treat him that way. Let us learn to lay down our lives, our preferences, our worldviews, and our cultures in pursuit of that which brings lasting love and encouragement. May we practice being promoters of true peace that makes space for others in love and mercy.

Prince of Peace, you are the gold standard to follow in pursuing harmony on the earth. Your example is a life of laid-down love. May I never forget that pride has no place in your kingdom, nor does false humility. As I look to you, teach me your peace-promoting ways.

In the Details

"He who is faithful in a very little thing is faithful also in much; and he who is unrighteous in a very little thing is unrighteous also in much."
LUKE 16:10 NASB

In the details and the mundane areas of our lives, we get to practice the character-building traits that we want to leave in our legacies. The things that most people never see mark our stories much more indelibly than the mountaintop highlights that some are privy to.

God is in the details. Do we value them as much as we do the big goals? If we will practice finishing the small things, we will be much more apt to follow through on the larger things in life. What areas have we been neglecting because we think they are insignificant? Ask God for perspective on these things and see what you can do about them.

Constant One, you are faithful in everything you do. I want to be like you. Show me the areas that I have been neglecting. Show me where I can receive your grace to be more like you. I know that you do not ignore the practical things. Teach me.

Out of the Boat

He said, "Come." And when Peter had come down out of the boat,
he walked on the water to go to Jesus.
MATTHEW 14:29 NKJV

Have you heard the Lord's voice inviting you to come to him? He bids you to bring him your worries and the heavy burdens you carry. He offers what no one else can. If you will step toward him, eyes fixed on his gaze, your feet will be steady, no matter what is underneath them.

Let go of the anxiety that holds you back from moving toward him today. He has rest for your soul, peace for your mind, and the joy of his presence to mend your heart. There is nothing you have need of that he does not offer you freely. Leave behind the comfort of your small boat and walk on the water of his great love that rises up to meet you.

Jesus, I fix my eyes on you right now. When I move toward you, will you also move toward me? I want to rest in the confidence of your goodness, leaving behind the anxiety that has descended upon my world. You are trustworthy. Here I am, answering your invitation.

Mercy Storehouse

We are citizens of heaven, where the Lord Jesus Christ lives.
And we are eagerly waiting for him to return as our Savior.
PHILIPPIANS 3:20 NLT

You belong to a kingdom that cannot be seen with the naked eye, but it is as real as the ground beneath your feet. The hope that you have set your life upon is not in vain; it is the strong foundation of God's love. Let your heart grow in expectation even as your sorrow deepens your need for his comforting presence.

Hold onto hope. God will meet you, even now, in the waiting. His Spirit is with you, and it is reassurance for the promises of his heart to all be fulfilled. Let him fill you with his great grace that empowers you to stand. You have access in this present moment to his storehouses of abundant mercy. It will feed your life in ways you cannot even imagine.

Father, I set all my hope on you and your faithful Word. You will not let me down. Meet me with the kindness of your heart and show me where you are working miracles of mercy in my life.

Peace that Lasts

"Let not your heart be troubled;
you believe in God, believe also in Me."
JOHN 14:1 NKJV

God is the giver of good gifts. He does not give to you with the expectation that you will offer him anything in return. He is a generous and merciful Father. Don't worry; he doesn't take back the gifts that he so freely gives away. You are his child, and as such, you never need worry about your needs being met.

The Spirit of God moves with the atmosphere of peace. He will not let fear overtake you. Invite him to reveal himself to you in a new way today. His revelations are like treasured gifts that impart the wisdom of his abundant heart of compassion. Rest in the peace he gives; the peace that lasts. Rest in him.

Holy Spirit, fill me with the kindness of your very near presence. Let your peace bring clarity and calm to my heart and mind. I want to rest in you today, in the confidence of your favor, knowing I could not drive you away. You are incomparably good.

Passionate Love

Christ proved God's passionate love for us by dying in our place while we were still lost and ungodly!
ROMANS 5:8 TPT

The love of God sees past our inadequacies and our failures to the inherent worth we have in him. He is a Father that loves his children more than life itself. He laid down his glory and came as a humble human to show us the way to live in perfect union with him. He did not spare even his own life but endured the humiliation of being put to death on a cross.

He knew the cost, and yet it was worth it to him to come. His passionate love propelled him, and it propels him today. He has not changed in his affection toward us, though we are fickle and hard to please. He is the best thing we will ever spend our lives on. Knowing him is the greatest reward.

Jesus, your love astounds me. The union of Father, Son, and Spirit is powerful and provocative. I want to know you more than I want to stay in my comfortable understanding of the world. I know that I only see in part, but you see fully. Reveal your passionate love to me in a new way today.

Not a Surprise

Do not be surprised at the fiery ordeal among you, which comes upon you for your testing, as though some strange thing were happening to you; but to the degree that you share the sufferings of Christ, keep on rejoicing, so that also at the revelation of His glory you may rejoice with exultation.

1 PETER 4:12–13 NASB

When troubles come, we should not be surprised. Life is full of opportunities to see God's faithfulness work itself out; he promised to never leave or forsake us. He also said that we should not be afraid but to be strong and take courage multiple times throughout his Word. There would be no need for such trust in God's unchanging character if our wills would not be tested by life.

There is a beautiful exchange that happens in our suffering; as we cling to God and understand that we get to share in what Jesus endured, he gives us his undeniable joy and peace that runs deeper than any trial or circumstance. His love will never be shaken. May we remain steadfastly looking to him through every storm. He is there.

Lord, when my world is shaking, may I see clearly that you are unmoved. You are always rich in mercy and patient in grace. I look to you now, waiting for you to reveal a new piece of yourself to me that I have not seen before. You are endlessly good.

Beautifully Humble

*He poured water into the basin, and began to wash the disciples' feet
and to wipe them with the towel with which He was girded.*
JOHN 13:5 NASB

This act of Jesus was a beautifully humble example of love poured
out. The King of kings knelt in the dust and washed the dirty feet of
his followers. He cleaned them with such service that exuded pure
love. The Lord over all did not require his disciples to do anything
that he wasn't willing to do.

By example he showed us how to love one another—to honor each
other the way God honors us. There are not some more worthy
than others to receive the pure compassion of God's heart. Do we
reflect this same kind of love in our lives? If not, how can we yield
our hearts to him and adjust the way we consider and treat others?

Humble Jesus, I am overwhelmed by the pure devotion you
showed your followers when you walked this earth. I am even
more overcome that you do the same with me. I want to be
like you in humility. Teach me. I will start with what I know to
do. Continue to lead and guide me in mercy.

In Every Moment

One who has unreliable friends soon comes to ruin,
but there is a friend who sticks closer than a brother.

PROVERBS 18:24 NIV

Though the ones we love may disappoint us in many ways, God never will. He does not lie, nor does he change his mind about us. No one can convince him out of his love. He is faithful and true, and he never leaves. He does not abandon us, ridicule us, or misunderstand our motives.

He is pure in compassion, and he is wholly aware of every part of our lives. He is for us. He is for our healing and our betterment. He is for our surrender because he knows the best way to guide us into life. He is a wonderful counselor, a reliable ally, and a forever friend. He is unmatched in his kindness and understanding. He is good. And he is close.

Holy One, all the words I have to describe you fall short in their impact. Language cannot define you, and my ideals can't contain you. You are better than I realize in every moment. Today, I yield to you. Come closer. Open my eyes and let me see where you are.

If the Lord Wills

*Instead, you ought to say, "If the Lord wills,
we will live and also do this or that."*
JAMES 4:15 NCV

There is security in walking closely with the Lord. When we submit our lives to him, he leads us in love. Even when we don't understand how anything good can come of suffering and sorrow, God works his redemptive love into our stories. There is not a tragedy that he will not bring goodness out of. If we let ourselves be transformed by the pain, God will use it to refine us.

There is no need to worry about what tomorrow will bring. God sees it all, and he knows just what we need right when we need it. Don't be afraid. Trust him today; he is able to do more than you can ask him to.

Lord, revive my heart with hope as I trust you. I will hold onto your unfailing character—your faithfulness and your love—like my life depends on it. When I am afraid, I will look to you. In your eyes, there is confidence.

Best Version

*As iron sharpens iron,
so a friend sharpens a friend.*
PROVERBS 27:17 NLT

Do you have the kind of friend who challenges you to be the best version of yourself? They don't need to constantly give you pep talks, but they see you, love you, and call out the goodness that is there. It is good to be with those who are willing to sit with you in your pain and not sugarcoat the reality.

True friends will hold up hope for us when we cannot do it for ourselves. Can you think of one or two people in your life that are like this? Perhaps reach out to them today and tell them what their friendship means to you. If you struggle to pinpoint a friend, ask the Holy Spirit to highlight one for you. Above all, he can be that friend to you. He is closer than any other.

Faithful Friend, you have shown me what it means to be a loyal and loving friend. Thank you for unrestricted fellowship with you. Thank you for flesh and blood friends too who encourage me and cover me. Help me to love them well, just as you love me.

Reality of Suffering

Since we are approaching the end of all things, be intentional, purposeful, and self-controlled so that you can be given to prayer.

1 PETER 4:7 TPT

On the hardest days, it can be difficult to see the forest for the trees. The overwhelming pain of loss can drown out every other thing. There is nothing wrong with you when you are overcome with sorrow. In those times, cry out to your Father who reads your every thought.

There is soberness in the reality of suffering, but there is always an opportunity to press into prayer. God is your help and your constant companion. He will not let you be consumed by what overcomes you. He is your shield and your guard. When you can do nothing else, look to him. He is not far away.

Constant One, you are who I rely on in both the good times and the awful. I know you will never leave me. When words fail me, read the cries of my heart. You are so attentive; run to me in my time of need and wrap me in your peace.

A Path Prepared

"Build up, build up, prepare the road!
Remove the obstacles out of the way of my people."
ISAIAH 57:14 NIV

God has knocked down every barrier that kept you from him. Today, there is nothing that separates you from his love. Nothing. Not failure, not sorrow, not doubts, nor disappointments. Nothing. You cannot convince him to leave you or try to talk him out of his love for you.

There is a path that leads straight to his kingdom, and you are already on it. He has built it up beneath you with the strong foundation of his unwavering mercy. He is so much better than you expect him to be. No one else can compete with his compassion. No one can outdo him in kindness, thoughtfulness, and relentless passion. Turn toward him today, and you will find that he is closer than you realized.

All Consuming One, I want to know the delight of your heart toward me. I am so quick to disqualify myself from your love, but I know that you never do! You have said I am worthy, so I will align my heart, my mind, and my life in your love again. I won't turn away and hide myself from you. Reveal yourself to me again.

Unaffected Goodness

"As for you, you meant evil against me; but God meant it for good, in order to bring it about as it is this day, to save many people alive."

GENESIS 50:20 NKJV

Not even the most ominous plans of the enemy, or of those who wish our downfall, can affect the goodness that God weaves into our lives. Even as we walk through the valley of the shadow of death, the Lord is closely leading us into his love. He sows his mercy into every portion of our stories. His unrelenting love cannot be stopped.

Let your heart take hope in God's constant compassion. He has not removed his favor from you. You are his, and nothing can change that. He will take even the most disastrous and devastating situations and still weave his love into it. If you cannot see it yet, keep going; you will. His restoration and redemptive work are not finished yet.

Good God, help me to believe that your goodness has not left me when I am overcome with sorrow. When I don't know what to do, you still do. Cover me with the shelter of your presence and keep me safe even as I mourn. I have to believe that I will see your goodness again in the land of the living. Don't fail me now!

October

Answer me when I pray to you,
my God who does what is right.
Make things easier for me
when I am in trouble.
Have mercy on me and hear my prayer.

PSALM 4:1 NCV

Bid for Connection

Because Your lovingkindness is better than life,
My lips will praise You.

PSALM 63:3 NASB

The love of God is indescribable in its depth, its breadth, and its intensity. Has it been a while since you experienced the delight, joy, and peace of his tangible affection? Let this moment be the opportunity you seize to ask for more. God is a good Father with an overflowing heart of kindness toward you. He will not turn away your bid for connection.

The Spirit of God fills us with the atmosphere of his great mercy. Time slows down and our hearts expand in the light of his radiant love. He is present; he is here in his fullness. There is more for us to taste, more for us to discover, and more for us to experience. His love is better than life.

Radiant One, flood me with your presence today. Awaken my senses to the nearness of your Spirit. Closer than the skin on my bones, you are with me. I'm hungry for more of you today, for the love that is better than any other.

Refreshing Waterfall

Anxiety weighs down the human heart,
but a good word cheers it up.
PROVERBS 12:25 NRSV

Encouragement is like a waterfall of refreshing water that washes over our hearts. It rinses the dust of disappointment from our souls as we remember that there is still good in our lives. There is still hope, and there is still more life to be had. God is not finished working his mercy into our stories.

Will you trade your worries and anxiety for the good Word that the Lord is offering you today? Give up what you cannot control and ask the Lord for his perspective. His wisdom sees what you cannot, and his heart can be trusted completely. Remember, he is the restorer. He is making all things new, and that includes you.

Good God, today I offer you every worry that fills my mind. I take hold of the good Word that you speak to me. I trust you with my heart and with my life. Speak Lord, for I am listening. Lead me in your love all the days of my life.

Intention and Action

God is the only Lawmaker and Judge.
He is the only One who can save and destroy.
So it is not right for you to judge your neighbor.
JAMES 4:12 NCV

God sees every detail in every person's life. He distinguishes intention from action and never misses even the slightest turn of a person's attention. He knows the deepest desires and motivations of every heart. He is the only one who can rightly judge, and he will do it.

The God who rescues is the same God who established everything by the law of his unrelenting love. He has not called us to declare judgment on anyone; rather he has called us to follow his example in extending mercy to others. Are our lives aligned in his love?

Righteous Judge, I confess that I have been quick to judge especially when I have taken offense at other people's lives and worldviews. I submit my heart to you and thank you for the mercy you so freely give. I will choose to extend the same to others today.

Rightly Qualified

It is not that we think we are qualified to do anything on our own.
Our qualification comes from God.
2 CORINTHIANS 3:5 NLT

There is no certification that needs to be obtained in order to follow God. There is no exclusive club to join in order to reap the benefits of his great favor and mercy. The kindness he offers is the same overwhelming love he offers to all people at all times.

Do you feel unqualified to share his love with others? Your life is your testimony, not someone else's. He has given you the same access to his wisdom that the greatest theologians have. He has qualified you, and that is all that matters. Stay humble, focus on Jesus, and follow his path of love and mercy. You have all you need to be what he has called you to be: a beloved child of God.

Father, how could I forget that I don't need to be more or do anything else to be completely accepted by you? You have called me, and you have called me out. I am worthy because you have said that I am. I will boldly live for you today.

In Every Promise

*Set your minds on things that are above,
not on things that are on earth.*

COLOSSIANS 3:2 NASB

There is a greater reality than what we can see with our natural eyes. The kingdom of God is not a far-off promised land, though we are not living in its fullness yet. Jesus taught us to pray that the Father's kingdom would come and be done on earth as it is in heaven.

There is more accessible to us through the kingdom of God on earth than we realize. When we set our hearts and minds on the things of God's kingdom, we will have greater perspective than the limitations of our current circumstances. God is always working, and his ways supersede our own. May we look to him, the author and the finisher of our faith, in every turn, in every problem, and in every promise.

Holy One, I know that your ways are higher than my own. Give me eyes to see your power at work in the world. I will not stop praying for your kingdom to invade the earth. You are better than I can imagine; I know it!

Unfaltering Delight

*"I am the Way, I am the Truth, and I am the Life.
No one comes next to the Father except through union with me.
To know me is to know my Father too."*

JOHN 14:6 TPT

In Jesus, there is perfect union with the Father. Through the Holy Spirit, we have fellowship with the triune God. What a wonderful mystery at work in our lives! When we start to waver in belief, may we fix our eyes on Jesus. He is the one who continually turns us back to the mercy-love of God.

There is nothing that keeps us from the love of God in Jesus. Nothing can steal his goodness from our lives. Even in our greatest hardships, God's persistent kindness covers us. His delight in us remains unfaltering, and the generosity of his mercy, resolute. He is worthy of our pursuit; we will never outdo him in love.

Wonderful Jesus, your affection is more amazing than anything I've ever known. Thank you for unhindered communion with you and the Father through your Spirit. I am undone. You are so good.

A New Facet

"Call to me and I will answer you,
and will tell you great and hidden things
that you have not known."
JEREMIAH 33:3 NRSV

If you have reached a point in your relationship with God where it feels stale, even forced, then let today be the day you're reminded that there is so much more to discover in him. In the book of Revelation, we see that even the elders who surround his throne have not reached the end of his glory. Every time a new facet of God's great character is revealed, they throw down their crowns before him and cry that he is worthy.

Call to him today, and he will answer you. He will reveal what you have never understood before. He is a faithful God, reliable to respond to his beloved ones. He is so much better, so much grander, than you now comprehend. Turn your attention to him, and you will not be disappointed by what you find.

Mysterious One, I long for a fresh revelation of who you are. I don't want to live off yesterday's bread. Give me a fresh portion today. Show me your glory, Lord! I want to see you as you are.

Silent Support

They sat on the ground with him for seven days and seven nights. No one said a word to him, because they saw how great his suffering was.

JOB 2:13 NIV

There is a beautiful solidarity in suffering when someone doesn't know what to say to offer respite or reprieve but will sit with us in our sorrow. Do you have those kinds of friends? The ones who will cry with you when you cry, feed you when you cannot cook for yourself, and hold you when words fail?

Though the trenches of grief are deep and feel isolating, there are friends who show up when it matters. May you know that kind of friendship; may you be that kind of friend. Know your people, the ones who are safe and who have your back. There is comfort in this kind of companionship.

Loving Lord, I know that you are with me through every dark night. Thank you for friends who also show up when it matters. I will lean on them when I have no strength of my own. May I not take for granted the support they offer. I see you even in this.

Strong Defender

*"You have also given me the shield of Your salvation;
your gentleness has made me great."*
2 SAMUEL 22:36 NKJV

God is the strong defender of your heart. He covers you with the shield of his salvation. He rescues you when you have no way out. He is your mighty deliverer, the liberator of your life. He has never left you, and he won't do it now. Though he is fiercely powerful to save, he is still gentle with you.

He leads you in kindness, no matter the situation. Even in correction, he is tenderhearted yet clear. He does not barter in shame or humiliate his children. He leads in love in everything he does. You can trust him with your heart; you can trust him with your life. He is good, and he is for you.

Mighty God, you are my Savior. You have rescued me over and over again. Don't stop now. Keep leading me in lovingkindness until all I see is you. I bind my heart to yours in loyal love; don't ever let me go.

Made Perfect

"My grace is sufficient for you, for power is perfected in weakness."
Most gladly, therefore, I will rather boast about my weaknesses,
so that the power of Christ may dwell in me.
2 CORINTHIANS 12:9 NASB

Your weakness is not a disqualifier. If you haven't already understood it, let it sink deep today: God's grace empowers you in strength. When you are weak, then God's power has more room to work. He will not let you down, and he certainly will not let you go.

The areas that you see as destitute, God sees as opportunities to work his marvelous restoration. His love is already moving on your behalf. You cannot fail him. Yield to his wonderful mercy; it is always generously flowing toward you. Let it carry you when you have nothing left to give. His power is made perfect in weakness.

Powerful One, I give in to the tide of your mercy. In your kindness, carry me through the storms that I cannot weather on my own. Why would I want to even try to get through in my own strength? I rely on you.

Song of Hope

We also have joy with our troubles,
because we know that these troubles produce patience.
And patience produces character,
and character produces hope.

ROMANS 5:3–4 NCV

If we let every circumstance teach us, we will find that our character grows in the light of God's faithfulness. There is not a trial or situation that we face, no matter how difficult or dark, that will keep us from growing in God. In fact, it is often in the deepest valleys, where we learn to lean on God in ways we never had to before, that we acquire tenacious trust.

Whatever you are going through, it is not without its opportunities. Will you let God build you in his love as unnecessary things fall to the wayside? You will not only make it out of this by the skin of your teeth; he will carry you through with a song of hope rising in your heart. You may not hear it yet, but its melody is already forming.

Faithful Father, I rely on you as much today as I ever have. Carry me when I have no strength to move on my own. Cover me when I am vulnerable and teach me what you will in the darkness of my night. Lead me in love, and I will know your goodness.

Cradled

*He heals the brokenhearted
and bandages their wounds.*
PSALM 147:3 NLT

There is no need to pretend to be whole when your heart is breaking. There is no reason to hide your sorrow and deep pain from the Lord or anyone else who loves you. He is closer than you realize. His love is wrapped around you, cradling you in his tender embrace.

He will not leave you untended; he is your healer, and he is right here. Do you trust that he can bind up the wounds in your heart? Do you believe that he can make you whole? Let his affection surround you as you listen for the gentle song he sings over you. He comes with healing and comfort. He rises with shining light to bring hope to the hopeless. Open up today and let the radiance of his love shine on you.

Healer, meet me in the midst of my deep pain and mend my broken heart. Soothe my soul with the melodies of your tender heart. I want to know you even in my deepest suffering. Come close.

A Wonderful Thread

We are convinced that every detail of our lives is continually woven together to fit into God's perfect plan of bringing good into our lives, for we are his lovers who have been called to fulfill his designed purpose.

ROMANS 8:28 TPT

There is not one single area of our lives left untouched by the wonderful thread of God's mercy. He weaves every detail together into a great tapestry of his grace. As lovers of God, we are marked by his persistent kindness toward us. As children of the Most High, we are covered by his goodness.

One day, when we look back on the scope of our lives, we will see that he brought beauty to even the darkest moments in our histories. He restores, he redeems, and he heals. Take heart today, for he is not finished with you yet. You will see the overwhelming lovingkindness of your good Father as plain as day.

Constant One, I know that you are always working on behalf of your children. You would not give up even if I were convinced you had. Thank you for faithfully loving me. I trust that you will work goodness into my life still. Let me see your kindness today.

Still on Course

The LORD will fulfill his purpose for me;
your steadfast love, O LORD, endures forever.
Do not forsake the work of your hands.
PSALM 138:8 ESV

There is no need to fear the future. It is in God's hands, and he knows what he's doing. Your suffering does not mean that you've gone off course. Wherever you are, there God is with you. Emmanuel. He never leaves, not even for a moment. He does not turn away, not ever.

Though you may look at your life through the deep pain of your sorrow and be unable to see what God could do with it, know that he is as faithful as he's ever been. Don't give up, especially don't give up your hope. He will never abandon you. Rest in his comfort and trust his reliable kindness. He won't fail you.

Lord, I lay aside every worried thought and all my anxiety about the future; you can have it! Fill my heart with confidence as I rest in you. I choose to trust you because you are worthy of it. Heal me with the balm of your presence.

Inseparable

In all these things we are more than conquerors through Him who loved us. For I am persuaded that neither death nor life, nor angels nor principalities nor powers, nor things present nor things to come, nor height nor depth, nor any other created thing, shall be able to separate us from the love of God which is in Christ Jesus our Lord.

ROMANS 8:37–39 NKJV

Read that passage again. Take your time, drinking in the message. There is nothing that will ever be able to separate us from the love of God. Not death, not life, not any beings or powers, not anything we face, not highest mountains or deepest seas, not any created thing. Nothing will ever come between us and the all-consuming love of God.

Consider the challenges in your life. Has fear convinced you that they are bigger than God? That somehow this would be the time when God doesn't come through? His mercy is relentless; you can't ever outrun it. He has been with you until now, and he will continue to be. Ground yourself in this moment. He is with you. Love surrounds you.

Eternal One, may the thoughts of my heart lead me back to you throughout this day. When I am tempted to think I am on my own or that the weight of my circumstances and pain will crush me, rush in with your tangible presence and remind me that I am united with you in love every single moment.

A Shared Life

The Spirit of the LORD will rest on Him,
The spirit of wisdom and understanding,
The spirit of counsel and strength,
The spirit of knowledge and the fear of the LORD.

ISAIAH 11:2 NASB

What wonderful news! We have the Spirit of the living God resting upon us—the same Spirit who filled Jesus. There is wisdom to know him more, and strength when we have run out of our own. There is power for every trial we face. It's all about communion with God.

Fellowship with the Lord is what it all comes down to. That we would know him, just as we are fully known by him. That we would love, rely, and communicate with him. That we would share our time, our attention, and our very lives with him. The same power that rose Christ from the dead is the power that is alive in us because of the Spirit. What a wonderful reality.

Spirit, I turn my attention to your presence with me now. Speak, for my ears are listening. Show yourself, for I am looking for you. I long to know you more—your wisdom, counsel, and strength. Teach me; I am your willing student.

Saturated

Let every activity of your lives and every word that comes from your lips be drenched with the beauty of our Lord Jesus, the Anointed One. And bring your constant praise to God the Father because of what Christ has done for you!

COLOSSIANS 3:17 TPT

There is so much beauty in the love of Christ. Remember what he has done for you already in your life. Let the memory move your heart in gratitude. Pour your heart out before him today. He is the same faithful and power-working God as he always has been.

Will you align your thoughts and life with his incomparable love today? Let his kindness be the measure you put every word against. The Spirit of God is your guide, leading you in love. Trust him, for he has not forsaken you. Your life is saturated by his mercy, and you will see his tangible goodness again. Lean into his presence today.

Loving God, I long to see your goodness clearly again in my life. Give my heart courage to keep pressing into you as you carry me through. I will not forget who you have shown yourself to be in my life; I trust that you are not finished with me yet.

Mighty Deliverer

The righteous person may have many troubles,
but the LORD delivers him from them all.

PSALM 34:19 NIV

God has not run out of rescues. He has not grown weary of saving his people from their troubles. He is known as the Mighty Deliverer, and that is still his name! What difficulties are you facing that you need God to deliver you from? Call out to him; he is a faithful help in times of trouble.

You can't tire God out with your requests. Don't fear the withdrawal of his love; it's impossible! He is with you through sun and rain, celebration and mourning. He is with you. Take hope today in the ability of God to save. He does not need your help, so it doesn't matter how helpless you feel. He will deliver you time and again, and he won't ever stop.

Mighty Deliverer, save me from my present troubles! I'm giving you all my worries and doubt; just come through for me again. Surround me with the hopeful expectation that your presence brings. Give me confidence as my heart links with yours in trust.

Restoration of Relationship

*Godly grief produces a repentance that leads to salvation
and brings no regret, but worldly grief produces death.*

2 Corinthians 7:10 nrsv

Godly grief shows us the disconnection we feel from God. Repentance leads us to salvation, and there is no regret there because there is unhindered connection with love. Godly repentance is after one thing: restoration of relationship.

When was the last time you felt disconnected from the heart of God because of choices you made? Instead of sitting in shame, when you repair the relationship with your honest vulnerability, there is freedom and life to be found. There is no risk of denial from God, for his love is always reaching toward you. Let his kindness lead you back to him again and again. That is the purpose of repentance.

Good God, I recognize areas of my life where I have kept your voice and opinion out. I want to be wholly influenced by your love. I yield my heart to you—every single part—and I ask for you to fill me with the light of your mercy again.

The Perfect Being

Answer me when I pray to you,
my God who does what is right.
Make things easier for me when I am in trouble.
Have mercy on me and hear my prayer.

PSALM 4:1 NCV

It is no small thing to ask for mercy. God makes it clear in the Scriptures that he is close to the humble, and he is their help. Whenever you call out to God, he hears you and he will answer you. He is the only righteous one—the only perfect being.

He who is perfect in love will not fail to extend his kindness to you. Seek and you will find. Knock and the door will be answered. Ask and you will receive. Don't hold back today. Whatever it is you need from God, ask him for it. He is quick in love and generous in mercy in every turn of your attention.

Ever-present One, hear my cries today and answer me. You know when I have run out of patience and strength, and you never shame me for it. Who else could love me to life over and over again the way you do? I won't hold back now. Come rushing in with your presence, like a waterfall of love.

No One Like You

No one is holy like the Lord!
There is no one besides you;
there is no Rock like our God.
1 Samuel 2:2 NLT

God's loving nature is not subject to change. His faithfulness is steadier than the earth beneath your feet. His constant mercy is more plentiful than the waters in the seas. He will never waver in his kindness toward his people. When our lives are built upon the foundation of his strong love, though the earth around us may shake, the bedrock of his love never will.

Consider the goodness of God and the holiness of his character. Can you find another who is like him in the earth? Even the most devout lover of God falls short, but God is perfect in every role he plays. He does not wander or waver. He is the same yesterday, today, and forever.

Holy One, there is no one else like you in all the world. When you speak, you always follow through on your Word. When you move, you do it in mercy and kindness. Your justice is unmatched, and your judgments pure and true. I trust you, for there is no one better to bind my life to.

Half the Weight

If one part suffers, every part suffers with it;
if one part is honored, every part rejoices with it.
1 CORINTHIANS 12:26 NIV

There is so much comfort to be found in sharing, both our joys and our disappointments, with others. A shared load is easier to bear. When we allow others to help carry the weight of our suffering and sorrow, the fellowship is reflective of what we have with Christ.

Who, knowing their friend was suffering deeply, would parade their joys in front of them without a care? Take notice of those who are sensitive to your current state. There is solace in knowing and meeting someone where they are. Will you allow those close to you to sit with you in your sorrow? Will you let them help lift the load?

Lifter of my head, I have known your present comfort in my life. Help me to let those who care for me do the same. I don't want to stay isolated in my pain. I will not bear it alone. Keep me soft to your comfort especially through those around me.

Test It

Do not believe every spirit, but test the spirits, whether they are of God; because many false prophets have gone out into the world.

1 JOHN 4:1 NKJV

You have the Spirit of the living God alive in you. You have the evidence of his fruit in your life. You have the wisdom of his Word available to you. Let those be your guide as you seek to discern different things in your life. Let the fruit of someone's life speak louder than their words.

You have not been given a spirit of fear. If fear is leading you, then you are not being led by the love of God. Remember, perfect love casts out fear. There is a difference between the awe and reverence you may call the fear of God, and the panic that leads to shutting down what is unfamiliar. Test the spirits, but do so with the tools that God has given you, not through blindly following another's lead.

Wise God, forgive me for my swift judgments of others when I have not done the work to discern the fruit that follows. I want to be quick in mercy, but I also want to be wise in how I live. Give me your perspective and continue to teach me.

Limited Energy

I will instruct you and teach you the way you should go;
I will counsel you with my eye upon you.

PSALM 32:8 NRSV

Do you feel lost in wondering what you should spend your limited energy on these days? Let the wisdom of God, who walks with you, lead you. The Spirit of God will counsel you as you spend time fellowshipping with him. Look into the Word, and you will find keys to help you.

You have a Counselor that is wiser than any other. You have a close friend who knows you better than you can imagine. Trust him to lead you. You may think you know what you should do, but he certainly knows what is best for you in this season. Will you let him lead you even if it is in a different direction than you thought you should go?

Shepherd of my soul, I trust you to guide me into your goodness. Show me the ways that I can love you well in this time when I don't have much to offer. Show me the best route through this hard season. I will not fight the simplicity you offer.

A Different Outcome

I pray with great faith for you, because I'm fully convinced that the One who began this glorious work in you will faithfully continue the process of maturing you and will put his finishing touches to it until the unveiling of our Lord Jesus Christ!

PHILIPPIANS 1:6 TPT

Have you ever looked at your life and wondered what happened? Did you think you would be further along by now? Did you have a completely different outcome envisioned? Take heart today, for God's ways are better than your own. He never stops leading in love, and his restoration power is always working for your good.

He has not lifted his hand of mercy from your life. You are completely covered by his compassion, and he is lovingly weaving his kindness into the fabric of your story. What sought to break you will be your rebirth. You will not ever be the same, but there is no need to be. You are growing up in the maturity of your faith. What is coming is beautiful, and what he is building is a powerful monument to his redemption. Just you wait and see!

Glorious One, thank you for the reminder of your redemptive power at work in my life. I trust that you haven't given up on me, and I will see your goodness as clear as day again in the land of the living. Awaken hope as I trust you in this process. I hold onto you.

Beyond Beautiful

"God so loved the world that he gave his one and only Son,
that whoever believes in him shall not perish but have eternal life."

John 3:16 NIV

When we go through seasons of stripping down, when loss knocks the wind out of our sails, hope can feel like a luxury of the past. No matter what is present or missing from our lives, there is a greater hope that transcends the realities of this short life. When we have reached the end of our walk on this earth, it is not the end, but a new beginning.

When we are the ones left behind, it can be a comfort to know that fellowship with our loved ones is not forever lost. There is an eternal, glory-filled, existence ahead of us. With the radiant light of the Son never setting, we will live in peace, finally and completely fulfilled by his wonderful mercy and love. It will be beyond beautiful. Take heart today.

Giver of life, give me a glimpse of your glory again today. Remind my soul that you are not limited in your love. I long for your living hope to embed in my very being, that I may be rooted and established in your mercy-kindness that promises eternal life.

Nature of Love

*Using the Scriptures, the person who serves God will be capable,
having all that is needed to do every good work.*
2 TIMOTHY 3:17 NCV

We are not left to work out our salvation on our own merit or in our own wisdom. We have a wonderful toolbox of keys to God's kingdom through his living Word. Search the Scriptures and you will find that God's beautiful character fills the pages.

Do you lack love? Look at the life of Jesus and be encouraged. Read through the letter to the Corinthians, where the nature of pure love is made clear. Whatever it is that you feel lacking in, there is evidence for obtaining through communion with the Holy Spirit. You have everything you already need. Seek him, and you will find him.

Spirit of God, enlighten the eyes of my heart as I read your Word. Give me revelation of your wisdom as I look for keys to life. Encourage my heart as I meditate on your Word today and lead me to deeper fellowship with you through it all.

Knit Together

Bear one another's burdens,
and thereby fulfill the law of Christ.
GALATIANS 6:2 NASB

When you think about the times you have felt most cared for, what is the overarching theme? Did friends and family show up for you in practical ways? Really think it through. What we value, we live out. The law of Christ has always been synonymous with the law of love.

When we bear one another's burdens, we share the weightiness of the load. There is so much kindness in sharing in each other's sufferings, and not just in other's joys. May our hearts be knit together, not shrinking back from conflict or pain, but pressing in with the love and kindness that we've been shown by Jesus. In this, we will fulfill the law of love that Christ has called us to.

Holy One, your requirements are not unattainable. When I am quick to make excuses for my apathy and indifference, pierce my heart with your present mercy. May it be a reminder of my calling to love others even when it's uncomfortable. I am grateful for those who have done the same for me. Keep my heart tender, Lord, as I walk with you.

Starting Fresh

By the help of your God, return;
Observe mercy and justice,
And wait on your God continually.
HOSEA 12:6 NKJV

Every new day is an opportunity to start fresh. It doesn't matter what yesterday looked like, or the failure of keeping it together even ten minutes ago. Walking with the Lord is not about perfection, it is about continually staying connected to his merciful heart.

Let this be the moment you breathe deeply of the presence of love. You have a choice in every waking instant to turn your attention to the kindness of God. Wait on him. Return to him. Cast all your cares on him. Pour out your heart before him without hesitation. Practice mercy and justice as much with yourself as with others. Surrender to his love and let yourself be renewed and refreshed in his presence.

Merciful God, help me to continually to turn back to you when I get distracted and off-track. You are better than my own intentions; I see that so clearly. I submit my heart, my mind, and my life to you again today. Lead me in your grace.

Stand for Justice

The LORD waits to be gracious to you,
and therefore he exalts himself to show mercy to you.
For the LORD is a God of justice;
blessed are all those who wait for him.
ISAIAH 30:18 ESV

Are you tired of waiting on God's justice? Are you trying to get it on your own terms and in your own way? Let him care for you, for you are his child and he knows best. It is not wrong to advocate for mercy and to stand up for justice. But be careful not to hand out your own judgment in the process.

Remember that the one who sees the motives of your heart is the one who sees the intention behind every person's actions. He will not stop being gracious to you, and he will never withhold his mercy from you. Will you align yourself in his kindness, standing for truth, no matter who stands against you? Continue to wait for him; his justice will not fail.

God of justice, rise up on behalf of your people. Do not let the brokenhearted be beaten down by the accusations and violence of the enemy. You are merciful; show mercy. You are just; bring justice. You are gracious; rain your grace over us.

I Need You

Lord, have mercy, because I am in misery.
My eyes are weak from so much crying,
and my whole being is tired from grief.

PSALM 31:9 NCV

When we have been worn down and don't have enough buffer to offer a smile to a stranger, let us remember that God does not require our happiness. There is a misery that comes with suffering: the pain of dark, lonely nights filled with gaping wounds of loss. God does not demand us to shake it off. He comes and sits close with us, surrounding us with comfort.

The merciful one draws near to us in our grief. He is not far away. When we are worn down, he covers us with lovingkindness. When we have nothing to offer, he gives us all we need. May we find rest and solace in his company. We are not alone.

Lord, have mercy when I am in misery. When my eyes are weak from all my crying, and my whole body is exhausted from grief, come close with the peace of your presence and sing songs of comfort over my heart. I need you, God. I need you.

November

Be faithful to pray as intercessors who
are fully alert and giving thanks to God.

COLOSSIANS 4:2 TPT

Mercy Remembered

The Living Expression became a man and lived among us!
And we gazed upon the splendor of his glory,
the glory of the One and Only who came from the Father
overflowing with tender mercy and truth!
JOHN 1:14 TPT

Have you forgotten what mercy looks like? If you struggle to remember its likeness, look at the life of Jesus, and you will find love personified. He is the embodiment of lovingkindness, and there is no one better than him. He humbled himself, leaving his glorious throne in heaven to become a human and live like us. He did it so we would know what God's nature is truly like.

His mercy and truth are unmatched in wisdom and understanding. He did not conform to our systems but showed us a better way— his higher truth. Jesus' life, death, and resurrection all point us to the unhindered fellowship that has always been God's heart for us.

Merciful One, thank you for the ability to know you. You cover me with your mercy and lead me into your heart with compassion. How could I not trade every burden for your love? You are so much better than life itself. Refresh me today in the reality of your goodness.

Transformed by Kindness

We all, with unveiled face,
beholding as in a mirror the glory of the Lord,
are being transformed into the same image from glory to glory,
just as by the Spirit of the Lord.

2 CORINTHIANS 3:18 NKJV

As we look to the Lord, we will find that the more time we spend with him, the more we begin to look like him. We cannot help but be transformed by his overwhelming love. As we receive his mercy in unending measure, we give out of the overflow of his nature to those in our lives.

This present season, along with its trials and troubles, will pass. It won't last forever. But even in the midst of pain and sorrow, we can be changed by the kindness that carries us. There is no pressure in this becoming, it is a natural consequence of being saturated by the love that sustains us. Turn toward the light of his radiant compassion; he is ever near.

Sustainer, I rely on you more than I even know. You are the one who carries me through the fiercest battles and shelters me in the violent storms of life. Keep me, and in my keeping, transform me by your love. I want to look like you.

Tuned In

Blessed be the Lord!
For he has heard the voice of my pleas for mercy.
PSALM 28:6 ESV

God is close. He hears every word that you speak, and he knows the thoughts of your mind. He is familiar with the timbre of your voice. Like a parent tuning into their child's cries, he always recognizes you. Do not shrink back in shame of what he finds in you; he knows you well, and he loves and accepts you unceasingly.

He will never turn away from your pleas for help. He does not ignore your whimpers. He is near with comfort, and he is at the ready, fighting on your behalf. There's no need to fear abandonment, for he will never leave you. He is more consistent than the rising and setting of the sun. He is more constant than the beating of your heart within your chest. Call to him; he is listening.

Near One, will you reveal your nearness to me again today? I need to know that you are with me. Take it past my logical understanding and hope, deep into my bones, into the knowing sense of your tangible presence. Meet me right where I am. I need you.

That Is It

Beyond all these things put on love, which is the perfect bond of unity. Let the peace of Christ rule in your hearts, to which indeed you were called in one body; and be thankful.

COLOSSIANS 3:14-15 NASB

When it all boils down, the law of love is the golden standard of God's kingdom. It is what remains, and it is what matters most. Whatever you do or don't do today, may you be wrapped up in the lovingkindness of God. Wear it like a cloak that covers you from head to toe.

There is unity within the love of God that sees past offenses and bonds hearts to one another. There is no greater pursuit in this life than to love God and to love others as we long to be loved. That is it. What areas of your life need to align in God's kindness? Submit them to him and let yourself be led by love.

Merciful Father, thank you for the reminder of what matters most in life. Cover me with your mercy and lead me in your love. Open my eyes to see the areas of my life where I have let offenses excuse my lack of love. I thank you that your love has no conditions. Help me to extend the same kindness to others as well as to myself.

Wonder of Creativity

Yours, LORD, is the greatness and the power and the glory and the majesty and the splendor, for everything in heaven and earth is yours.
1 CHRONICLES 29:11 NIV

Have you ever looked at the bright stars in the sky, overwhelmed by the scope of the universe? Have you encountered things in nature that made you feel insignificant in comparison? There is so much beauty and grandeur in the world around us: things that were here long before we were and will long outlast us.

All of these belong to the Creator. He imagined them and spoke them into existence. And he is the same one who breathed life into you. Have you felt the wonder of his creativity at work within you? You are a masterpiece of his workmanship: more valuable to him than the grandest sights you could find in this earth.

Maker of heaven and earth, awaken the wonder in my heart today at who you are. Your creativity is astounding, and your care even more so. You do nothing by accident. Thank you that I am a reflection of that. Open my eyes to the wonder of your glory.

Heart Medicine

A joyful, cheerful heart brings healing to both body and soul.
But the one whose heart is crushed
struggles with sickness and depression.
PROVERBS 17:22 TPT

We cannot escape times of deep mourning and grief. We cannot avoid suffering in this life. God never promised us that we would. He did, however, promise to never leave us alone. He promised to comfort us, to sustain us, and to rescue us. In the life of Jesus, we see that he wept with those who wept, and he celebrated with those who were filled with joy.

He is not asking us to pretend that what is crushing our souls is not that bad. He is near to the brokenhearted. The psalmist declared that over and over again. He is near to those who are crushed in spirit. He brings comfort, and he also brings healing. We may not like the process of pain that brings us to our healing, but God is in even that. Do we trust that he is still good?

Comforter, be near in the deep pain of my grief. Minister your comfort to my broken heart and make me whole in your love. I submit myself to you in this process. I believe that you are with me and that you will tend to and mend me in your kindness.

Help Always

In the same way the Spirit also helps our weakness;
for we do not know how to pray as we should,
but the Spirit Himself intercedes for us
with groanings too deep for words.

ROMANS 8:26 NASB

When words fail us, and we do not know what to do or what to say, our moans become our prayers. In the depths of our pain, our cries call out to the Father of love who hears us. The Spirit himself intercedes on our behalf, knowing just what we need even when we don't.

When you are at a loss for what to pray, know that the Spirit already sees and understands your heart. As deep calls to deep, as the psalmist says, so spirit cries out to Spirit. There is no limit to the help that God gives us through the fellowship of his presence. He is your help at all times and in all ways.

All-knowing One, I know that you hear the cries of my heart. You know what is behind my groans even when I don't understand them. Don't stop meeting me in the messiness of this suffering season. You are my help, and I rely on you.

A Necessity

All who have entered into God's rest have rested from their labors,
just as God did after creating the world.
HEBREWS 4:10 NLT

Are you tired today? Are you weary of holding it together for others while internally you feel as if you are falling apart? There is an invitation to real rest for you today—the kind that does not require you to do anything or to be anyone you're not in this moment.

Will you lay down the burdens and expectations you have for yourself, as well as what others have of you, and let the peace of God lead you to rest? Maybe you are thinking of how much there is to get done today and the obligations you can't get out of. What if you used the moments that you have available to lay down all expectations and just do what feels necessary? Rest is not a luxury; it is a necessity. Make it a priority, and then let yourself let go of everything else in that time.

God, help me to prioritize rest when I can and not feel guilty when I follow your example in this. Thank you that I don't need to be productive at all times. Show me ways where I can incorporate rest into my life as a practice. Teach me to let go.

Not Easily Swayed

My covenant I will not break,
Nor alter the word that has gone out of My lips.
PSALM 89:34 NKJV

God always keeps his promises. Though he does not work on our timelines, he never strays from his Word. We can trust him, and we can trust his timing. He is good, and that never changes. When we are walking through deep pain and suffering, it can feel as if all goodness has abandoned us. But that is not true. God, in his steadfast kindness, is with us and working his restorative love into every fiber of our stories.

What God says, he does. He is not fickle or easily swayed. His generous mercy is always flowing over our lives even when we cannot sense it. He is faithful, he is constant, and he is unrelenting in love.

Faithful Father, breathe your courage into my heart again today. Remind me of your faithful love that has never left me. I have seen your goodness at work before, and I trust that I will clearly see it again. Revive my hope as you faithfully lead me.

Goodness Stored

How abundant are the good things
that you have stored up for those who fear you,
that you bestow in the sight of all,
on those who take refuge in you.

PSALM 31:19 NIV

What a wonderful encouragement: goodness is not scarce in the kingdom of God. He is always generous in love, and he has stored good things for those who look to him. There is abundance in his heart, and he will not fail to pour it out on us.

Take refuge in him today; let him pull you close to his steadfast love as he surrounds you with the peace of his presence. He is so very near even now. He will not cut you off from his kindness. You have access to all you could ever dream of and so much more! He is more than enough, and he won't stop planting seeds of his goodness in your life.

Good God, in your abundance I find all that I need. Pour your Spirit's peace over my mind and fill my heart with your tangible love that I may have the clarity that comes with your presence. I long for more of you today.

On His Mind

*"See, I have written your name on my hand.
Jerusalem, I always think about your walls."*

ISAIAH 49:16 NCV

God could not forget his people. Though we may forget those we've left behind or those who are no longer in our lives, God is not confined to our limitations. Unfailing in love, he always remembers us. He remembers every person who has ever called on his name.

Your life is not a trivial matter to God. You are incredibly important to him. Have you forgotten the depths of his love and mercy? They know no end. You are seen and known by the Creator of all things. He carefully knit you together in your mother's womb and filled your lungs with breath. You are his. You belong to him. And you are on his mind.

Father, it is almost too much to imagine that you would think of me. Not that you are fleetingly thinking about me, but that you know every detail of my life and heart, and you love me fiercely. I am in awe. What do you have to say directly to me today?

Help for All

God, hurry to help me, run to my rescue!
For you're my Savior and my only hope!
PSALM 38:22 TPT

God is not the Savior of the select few. He is Savior to all. Jesus' sacrifice on the cross was not simply for his disciples or for the people of that time. It was for all of us, everyone who has ever lived and breathed and walked this earth. He is a help to everyone who calls on his name today.

Today is the day of your salvation. If you have run out of time or of ways to get through, God is your ready help. Cry out to him. He will not delay. If your only hope is in him, double down and throw it all on him again. He will not fail you.

Savior, I trust that you will not let me be destroyed by the things in life that seek to crush me. I need you. Come to my help today, for I cannot wait another moment for relief. Don't turn away from my cries for help; I have nothing, no hope, without you. Come through for me again.

Special Merit

You are a chosen generation, a royal priesthood, a holy nation,
His own special people, that you may proclaim the praises of Him
who called you out of darkness into His marvelous light.

1 PETER 2:9 NKJV

You were chosen as God's own before you had any idea about who he was. Jesus himself qualified you; you didn't do anything to gain special merit in his sight. When you remember your life before knowing him, what differences do you see from then until now?

How has knowing God changed you? Has being known by him and following in his example transformed your life in any way? His marvelous light shines on all who fellowship with him. Come alive in the revelation light of his kindness and overwhelming goodness again today. Every moment is a new opportunity to know him more.

Father of love, it is astounding to me that you not only think of me, but you chose me as your own. I won't ever get over the kindness of your heart. Reveal yourself to me in a new way as I reflect on your indescribable love and power.

Intent on Knowing

*"You will seek me and find me
when you seek me with all your heart."*

JEREMIAH 29:13 NIV

When was the last time you really sought God? Was there a question that would not leave you until you knew its answer? Was there a facet of his character that you'd caught a glimpse of that you just could not shake until you saw more of it?

God clearly says in his Word that those who look for him will find him. Is your heart intent on knowing him more? Here is yet another opportunity for you to press into the wonderful kindness of God who is always reaching out in love. When you seek him, really wanting to find him, he will reveal himself. Revelations of his goodness come to those who look for him.

Lord, I want to know you more. I have tasted and seen your goodness in my life before, but I long for more revelations of your nearness. Will you reveal yourself to me in a new way as I look for you in my life?

Dig Your Heels In

*Blessed is the one who perseveres under trial because,
having stood the test, that person will receive the crown of life
that the Lord has promised to those who love him.*

JAMES 1:12 NIV

There is no lack of opportunity in life to learn to dig our heels into tenacious trust of God. Life is sure to test us. When it does, do we throw up our hands and give up? Or do we persevere in faith? Sometimes perseverance looks like continuing to put one foot in front of the other. It whispers when we have no energy to shout.

Perseverance doesn't feel like confidence at all times. It doesn't look like perfection either. It is the resolute decision, over and over again, to keep going even with doubts and questions in tow. We don't have to know exactly where it will take us to decide to keep moving, doing the next right thing when it's in front of us. Just don't give up. Keep on following the voice of love.

Constant One, I will follow where you lead me. And when I don't know where to go or what to do, I will take the next step available. Even though I can't see the end of this trial, I will keep going, trusting that you will continue to guide me in truth.

Lovingly Devoted

I am praying to you because I know you will answer, O God.
Bend down and listen as I pray.

PSALM 17:6 NLT

Is God's faithful nature your foundation? No matter what has come before, his love is always available in abundance. Turn to him once again and pour out your heart. He not only hears you, but he responds in kindness.

If your picture of God is of a distant grandfather figure, one who comes in and out of your life, can you evaluate why that is? Don't be afraid of your questions. God is not apathetic toward you or any other. He is a lovingly devoted Father who knows you better than you know the back of your hand. Call out to him and wait for him to respond.

Father, I yield my heart to you again. As I pour out my misgivings, my disappointments, my needs, and my hopes, will you come close with your peaceful presence? Speak to me, for your words are life to my soul.

Your Praise

Heal me, O Lord, and I will be healed;
Save me and I will be saved,
For You are my praise.
JEREMIAH 17:14 NASB

There is no one better than Jesus. His lavish and loyal love is pure in its essence and unrelenting in its capacity and pursuit. His mercy is without blemish. He gives freely of his grace to all who look to him. He never turns away from the needy, but he draws close to the brokenhearted.

God is full of compassion that covers every mistake we could ever make. He does not hold our errors against us. He is quick to forgive and he is more patient than any other. He is Healer, he is Savior, and he is Redeemer. Whatever good you find in your life is a gift from the Father of love. Let him be your praise today.

Lord, you are the giver of all good gifts. I will praise you, for you have not abandoned me in my despair and sorrow. You have been my comfort and my stronghold when the winds and waves crashed over me. You would not let me go. I am so thankful. Continue to heal and save me as I depend upon your mercy.

No Parameters

Jesus, when He came out, saw a great multitude and was moved with compassion for them, because they were like sheep not having a shepherd. So He began to teach them many things.

MARK 6:34 NKJV

Do you feel lost in the waves of grief? Has all that once felt secure been tossed around, leaving you confused as to where to go and what to do? Jesus is your good shepherd, and he will not leave you to be thrown about by the chaos of the storms you face.

His compassion for you goes deeper than you realize. He does not put parameters on his love—not ever! Where you are, his love reaches and covers you. You cannot escape the grip of his marvelous grace. He holds you, and he will keep you safe. Listen for his whisper; his voice will instruct and teach you. He is near.

Good Shepherd, continue to guide me in your love. Move my heart with the tenderness of your presence that pulls me in with peace. I long to hear your voice again, teaching me with your wisdom and soothing me with your comfort. I rely on you.

Moving in Love

My child, give me your heart,
and let your eyes observe my ways.
PROVERBS 23:26 NRSV

There is no better parent than God. He is perfect in his motives toward us, knowing us better than we know ourselves. He is trustworthy. We can depend on his kindness to guide us into his goodness. Even through suffering, he is near with his ever-present comfort.

When we allow God to have our hearts, he heals what we didn't even know was broken. He mends the wounds that we kept hidden, not knowing how to heal them ourselves. As we follow in his footsteps, we find that his law is full of lovingkindness, leading us into life. He will not fail us. What feels like the end is not. He is still moving in love.

Good Father, I trust you with my heart. You can have access to every part, for you are good and you are working for my good. Heal me with the salve of your presence and give me eyes to see where you are moving in love. May my eyes stay fixed on you, for you never change.

Asking Again

*I begged the Lord three times
to take this problem away from me.*

2 CORINTHIANS 12:8 NCV

Do not hold back your requests from God. There is nothing wrong with asking him for the same thing over and over again. But also make sure to leave room for him to speak to you. Is your faith in what God gives, or is it in who he is? There is no need for pretense in your relationship with the Lord. He already knows what is in your heart. Cast all your cares on him, for he cares for you.

Though we may not always receive what we want, he always provides what we need. When we remember his great goodness, the mercy he pours over us without measure, may our hearts yield to his own in surrender and trust. Though we may be prone to doubt, he is confident. We can rest in that confidence today.

Lord, you already see through the exterior I present to others. You know what's really going on in my heart. I won't hold back from you today. Here it is, all of it. Meet me in it and lead me to ask you once again.

Already Working

He will care for the needy and neglected
when they cry to him for help.
The humble and helpless will know his kindness,
for with a father's compassion he will save their souls.

PSALM 72:12-13 TPT

What are you feeling today? What are the thoughts ruminating in your mind? May you remember the power of your God and the gentle compassion with which he meets you. If you feel helpless, there is good news. God is your advocate and your help. If you feel humbled beyond belief, take heart. God is all the strength you need, and he is already working on your behalf.

Cry out to him for whatever help you need. He is close, beloved, ever so close. He will not turn away from you; today is the day of your salvation, not your abandonment. He will never leave you. Never! He is rising up for you, and you need only trust him.

Savior, I rely on your help more than I ever have. Don't disappoint me. I choose to rest in your loyal love; cover me with the peace of your presence and do what only you can do in my life. Bring restoration, Lord.

The Helper

"The Helper, the Holy Spirit, whom the Father will send in My name,
He will teach you all things, and bring to your remembrance
all that I said to you."
JOHN 14:26 NASB

The promise that Jesus made to his followers about the Holy Spirit's presence and help is our inheritance. The Holy Spirit's power is not reserved for a special few, nor is his presence isolated to a rigorous process of selection. He is the promised helper for all who know Jesus.

When was the last time you sensed the Holy Spirit's work in your life? If you struggle to know whether you ever have, look at the fruit of the Spirit. In areas where these are present, there is the presence of God's Spirit in your life! Wherever there is love, joy, peace, patience, kindness, goodness, faithfulness, gentleness, and self-control, it is evidence of his work in you.

Holy Spirit, give me eyes to see where you are and have been at work in my life. I'm thankful for your aid whenever I need it. I know I am not alone in this life. Teach me your wisdom and remind me of the indescribable goodness of loving and being loved by you.

Keep Running

Since we are surrounded by so great a cloud of witnesses,
let us also lay aside every weight, and sin which clings so closely,
and let us run with endurance the race that is set before us.

HEBREWS 12:1 ESV

What has been holding you back from running with freedom in life? Are there things that you've held onto that no longer serve you well? Are there habits or old ways of thinking that keep pulling you back to what feels like the starting point over and over again?

Take heart; you are not running a solo race in an isolated place. You are surrounded by those who have gone before you, and they are cheering you on. You have not reached the end yet, and there is more freedom for you. Will you lay aside the weight of other's expectations, as well as the shame of sins that keep you cycling into despair? There is more for you here.

Holy One, help me to throw off the things that I have been carrying for far too long that don't help me run with freedom. I want to be free in you, and I know I'm not the only one who has struggled. Encourage me with the testimonies of others who have already tread this path.

The Full Picture

A thousand years in your sight
are like a day that has just gone by,
or like a watch in the night.
PSALM 90:4 NIV

In troubles and suffering, it can be hard to see past the darkness of the pain that closes in around us. There is something about grief that makes our little lives seem even smaller. But there is one who sees the big picture at all times. He doesn't miss a detail, but he also never loses his perspective that takes everything in at once.

Will we trust the one who has led us this far? He will not quit fulfilling his promises; his faithfulness has not run out. He is working all things together—even the pain of our present suffering—into the redemptive story of his unending love. He is powerful to save, and he will not give up on his Word.

Faithful God, I believe that you are still working your mercy into my life as powerfully as you ever have. Give me tenacity to hold onto hope even when this suffering season feels like an endless night. I know that the intensity will pass. Cover me in compassion in the meantime.

A Sound Mind

God has not given us a spirit of fear,
but of power and of love and of a sound mind.
2 TIMOTHY 1:7 NKJV

The power of a sound mind is found in the revelation-light that God gives. He instructs us with his wisdom, and our minds align with his truth when we submit our thoughts to him. He renews us with the transformation of our minds. There is no fear of punishment in his love. There is power for the revival of all things.

Let what has kept you back from going after God fall to the wayside as you drink in the purity of his presence today. His wisdom brings light to even the most complex problems we face. There is no difficulty that is too much for him to handle. Give him your attention today and let him transform your mind with his truth.

Great God, you are full of wisdom and insight. Renew my mind as I fix my thoughts on you today. You are better than the best news this world has to offer. You are full of lovingkindness and confidence. I set my eyes on your beautiful character.

No Striving

*"If in my name you ask me for anything,
I will do it."*
JOHN 14:14 NRSV

Have you grown weary of petitioning God? Are you tired of asking him for what feels unattainable? Why not let him lead you today. Slow down, take a deep breath, and focus your mind on the truth of his nearness. There is no striving in his love.

Before you ask him for anything today, remember who he is. Remember his kind affection toward you, his open heart of mercy that reaches out to you. Remember his greatness that the heavens and earth cannot contain. When you have a clear picture of his kindness, then ask for anything and listen for his response. Let your heart reach out in fellowship, seeking the give and take of relationship.

Wonderful Jesus, you are a better friend than any I've ever known. You are consistent in kindness and generous in understanding. Give me eyes to see you as you are today. I want to know you and your steadfast love more than I want to just get by. Answer me in your mercy.

Total Fulfillment

They desire a better, that is, a heavenly country.
Therefore God is not ashamed to be called their God,
for He has prepared a city for them.
HEBREWS 11:16 NKJV

When you dig under the surface of your desires, what is at the core of them? Underneath the longing for companionship, for comfort, and for provision, what is it that rings truer? There is a deeper aching for a better life, a better kingdom, a better world, than we now inhabit.

There is beauty in the glimpses we catch of God's wonderful kingdom come to earth as it is in heaven. But they are just hints of the greater glory awaiting us. The foretaste of overwhelming love that covers every sin and shame, and the peace that sets every heart to rest, is sweet, if fleeting. May we set our eyes on things above and remember that what is coming is greater than the things we leave behind.

Desire of every nation, you are the complete picture of hope. I look to you for every cue and for the fulfillment of every longing. Without you, I have nothing. In you, I feel expectation grow as I look forward to dwelling in freedom in your eternal kingdom.

Even Lions

Even lions may get weak and hungry,
but those who look to the LORD will have every good thing.

PSALM 34:10 NCV

God has promised to provide for the needs of his children. As his own, there is no reason to give over to the worry of what will become of us. He leads us in kindness and will provide for every need we have. Those who look to him will lack no good thing. We have all we need in him right now.

When was the last time you felt truly satisfied? Be honest, and do not be ashamed of the answer. Whatever it is, and however long it has been, there is exactly what you need in his presence today. Invite the Spirit of the living God to minister to your deep longings; he will not turn you away. He is faithful and true, and he is with you.

Lord, fill me with the satisfaction of your abundant life today. I long for a refreshing touch from you. Encounter my heart with the glory of your great affection. I need you. Meet me with grace.

Dream Big

> *"No eye has seen, no ear has heard,*
> *and no mind has imagined*
> *what God has prepared*
> *for those who love him."*
>
> 1 CORINTHIANS 2:9 NLT

When was the last time you dreamed big about the goodness of God? Imagine the most extravagant love and kindness you have ever known. The length of God's love is even greater, even longer, even more powerful than the small glimpses you have seen.

There is so much goodness in store for you yet. Run into the open arms of your delighted Father today and find the pure joy of his heart over you—his beloved child. Let your heart be awakened to the hope of his living love that heals, restores, and encourages. You are the object of his affection. Come alive in his love today.

Wonderful Father, your love is better than life! Fill me with the tangible joy of your presence. Awaken my heart to your living love and flood my thoughts with the clarity of your wisdom. You are incomparable. Pour out your Spirit again and revive my weary heart.

Reign of Grace

Remember this: sin will not conquer you, for God already has! You are not governed by law but governed by the reign of the grace of God.

ROMANS 6:14 TPT

There is no need to fear a takeover of sin or shame over your life, for you have been called by grace and covered in the compassion of God's powerful love. Remember whose you are today. Christ already victoriously defeated every aspect of death, and nothing can separate you from the reign of his grace over your life.

The God of abundant mercy calls you his own. He is your covering, your defender, and your final word. Nothing can snatch you from the grip of his love. There is no need to fear. Let confidence arise within you as you look to the victor, Jesus Christ. He is your salvation. He is your shield. You are not governed by laws that diminish; rather, you are ruled by the law of God's lovingkindness.

Gracious One, would you overcome every dark thought with the light of your life today? I know that fear is not my master, and my mistakes don't define me. You do. You are my guiding light.

December

The LORD is close to everyone

who prays to him,

to all who truly pray to him.

PSALM 145:18 NCV

Hasten the Day

"Glory to God in the highest,
and on earth peace among those with whom he is pleased!"
LUKE 2:14 ESV

We cannot escape the love that God pours over us. His presence is permeated with peace. May we be saturated in the pure compassion of his heart that puts our anxieties to rest. He is worthy of our trust. With our whole hearts submitted to him, we are clothed in the beauty of his affection. We cannot escape the purity of his purposes for us.

As an offering of adoration, let us join with the angels and proclaim, "Glory to God in the highest!" The first coming of Jesus, in flesh and bone, was a beautiful picture of the humility of his love. His second coming will bring with it the clear power of his glory on display for all to see. May he hasten the day as we dwell in his peace.

Great God, breathe peace into the depths of my heart and make every chaotic worry come to rest as I trust in your unchanging goodness. You are powerful to save, and I know that you aren't finished with your work in this world. Lead me into rest as I reflect on your great glory.

Finding Belonging

*"All that the Father gives Me will come to Me,
and the one who comes to Me I will certainly not cast out."*
JOHN 6:37 NASB

We are welcomed into the family of God with open arms. There are no hoops to jump through in order to receive his lavish mercy. We have been called by name by the giver of life itself. He created us, knows us, and calls for us to follow him.

When we walk the path of love that Jesus leads us on, we will not be led astray. With submissive hearts, we join our lives with his, and he pours out everything we need through fellowship with his Spirit. Jesus never turns away the needy, and he's not about to start doing it now. Come to him and find the belonging that your soul has always longed for. He is good.

Jesus, I come to you with all I have and the lack that I feel so acutely. I know that your requirements are few. I want to know you in spirit and truth, following along your pathway of peace all the days of my life. Lead me in your love, and I will follow.

An Open Book

All my longings lie open before you, LORD;
my sighing is not hidden from you.

PSALM 38:9 NIV

There are no mysteries to God. He sees you as you are, and he accepts you fully. He knows the longings of your heart, and the way it aches with yearning. He does not tire of your hopes, though you may long to disconnect from them yourself.

Your life is like an open book before him. Will you let him lead you into life? Though you experience sorrow and suffering, God is with you in it, weaving his mercy into every detail of your story. When you let him guide you, you will not be disappointed in the end. He has a way of making even the darkest night a garden full of sweet fruit, though you may not see the fullness of its beauty until the daybreak of a new season.

Loving Lord, I will follow you, trusting your steady hand to guide me when I cannot see. Though darkness surrounds me, and I cannot clearly distinguish what is hiding in the shadows, I know that you see it all so very clearly. Heal me as I lean on you. Do what only you can do. Redeem everything.

This Present Moment

This is the day the Lord has made;
We will rejoice and be glad in it.
Psalm 118:24 NKJV

Today is a new opportunity to slow down, release the regrets of yesterday, and focus on where God meets you in the here and now. Let tomorrow's worries go, as you drink in the gift of this present moment. There is peace to be found here. There is love to receive. There is joy to unearth.

As you go throughout this day, try focusing on what is in front of you. Whether it be the crisp air outside, the warmth of a pet as they lean into you, or the shoulder of a loved one, ground yourself in the present. Breathe in and feel the air in your nostrils. Breathe out and feel the sensation of letting go of the past moment. There is beauty to be found in this day. Will you look for it?

Good God, help me to be grounded in the present, not reaching back for yesterday or leaning ahead into the future. I want to taste and see your goodness and kindness in the day that I am living right now. Help me to find gladness in the small things.

This Simple

"Love the LORD your God with all your heart, all your soul,
all your strength, and all your mind."
Also, "Love your neighbor as you love yourself."

LUKE 10:27 NCV

There is no higher law than the law of love. Jesus summed up the intent behind the Old Testament law when he said to focus on loving God and loving others. It is actually that simple. If we choose to honor others the way that we desire to be honored, and we love the Lord with all that we have, we are doing the will of God.

Have you gotten caught up in issues that distract you from the call to love? If you have, there is fresh mercy to realign you in God's ways today. Love is not a feeling, nor is it simply a superficial act. Love is a lifestyle of choosing to offer mercy to others with no strings attached. Love is a lifestyle of submission to God. It does not require perfection; it is all about unhindered connection. Will you choose to walk the path of laid-down-love?

Merciful One, thank you for unending love that covers all my missteps. Realign my vision today so I see you, and I walk in your ways of humble love that seeks to serve others. Keep my heart in yours so my motives remain pure. And when they aren't, kindly lead me to repentance.

Back Then

Let what you heard from the beginning abide in you.
If what you heard from the beginning abides in you,
then you will abide in the Son and in the Father.
1 JOHN 2:24 NRSV

Sometimes, the best thing we can do is go back to the beginning, when things were simple and clear. What was it like when you first started walking with the Lord? What did it look like to abide? What was clear to you then that now seems less so?

There is wisdom in maturity, but there is also purity in innocence. There is beauty in both. Can you embrace the complexity you feel now while also remembering the simplicity of what God actually requires? He doesn't need you to save anyone. He doesn't need your help. And yet, he delights in your willingness to reach outside of yourself in love. Let him love you to life again today, as you abide in his Word and his Spirit abides in you.

Wonderful Lord, take me back to the start when you first wooed me with your love. Let me remember the awe I felt as I first learned to hear your voice. Life with you has always been about abiding; fellowship is what you've always wanted. I yield my heart to you again today as you surround me with compassion.

Get Up Again

The godly may trip seven times, but they will get up again.
But one disaster is enough to overthrow the wicked.

It doesn't matter how many times you trip and fall, love lifts you back up every time. The fact that you are still here, you are still going, means that you have not reached the end. Do not fear failure, for it will not define you. God, in his mercy, meets you each new day with overflowing kindness.

The success of your life is not dependent on your own ingenuity or strength. In suffering, when your confidence is stripped away and a comfortable existence seems like a fantasy, you can know the overwhelming love and power of your good Father. His strength is better than your own. His wisdom is all encompassing. Lean into his love again today and let him lift you up.

Faithful One, thank you for the reminder that it doesn't matter how far-gone I feel, you are still with me. Lift me when I have no strength of my own to stand. Carry me when my legs give out beneath me. I will keep going, for you are the one who leads me in lovingkindness.

A Simple Pursuit

"Whatever you ask in prayer,
believe that you have received it,
and it will be yours."
MARK 11:24 ESV

Faith is a simple pursuit. It is placing all of our confidence in the unchanging nature of the one who created us from dust. It is putting all our hope in God's mercy and his faithful kindness in following through on every promise that he has made. It is not blind trust; it is deeply rooted in the love of our good Father.

Today, as you present your requests to God, will you remember his nature? He pours into us the shining light of his revelation and speaks his clear wisdom to our hearts when we seek to understand him. His perspective is pure; let your faith be rooted in the faithfulness of God, and not in your own shifting desires.

Giver of Life, I remember today that I am not wishing on a star when I cry out to you. Your answer is not a vain hope, but a sure thing. You never withhold your love from those who seek you. I won't stop seeking you today; answer me and come close. Encourage me in your presence.

The Perfect Standard

*I want you to pattern your lives after me,
just as I pattern mine after Christ.*
1 CORINTHIANS 11:1 TPT

When we don't know what to do, may we look to the life of Christ. In him is the perfect standard of loving pursuit. We cannot go wrong if we line up our lives with his. We will not end in a dead-end of despair if we choose to show mercy and kindness to others.

Let us also remember that Jesus spent time advocating for those others looked down upon. There was none so humble in life that he would not extend kindness toward them. He healed those who society had outcast. He hung out with sinners and broke bread with those whom the religious elite deemed unfit. As we live our lives, may we be aware of where our kindness extends and where it doesn't. And then, may we choose greater love every opportunity we get.

Loving Lord, your example of service and love is a humbling one to follow. Remind me what matters when I forget. Let my life be lined with your mercy, love, and grace.

Liberated

*There is now no condemnation
for those who are in Christ Jesus.*
ROMANS 8:1 NASB

There is a clean slate before you today. There is nothing that has happened in your life, no choices you have made, that exclude you from receiving God's mercy. If you are in Christ, you are a new creation. He does not condemn you, nor does he deal in shame.

Let the guilt of your past lift off as you look to Jesus, the author and finisher of your faith. It is his mercy that covers you. It is his kindness that leads you. Let go of the regrets you have held onto and receive the light load of God's affection. He is full of delight over your life. Will you let love's light shine on your open heart today?

Savior, you are my liberator. You have freed me from guilt and shame. I lay all my mistakes before you along with the regrets that I've been replaying in my mind. I want my eyes to be fixed on your mercy so fully that everything else drifts off in the tide of your righteousness. You have made me clean, so I am clean.

Harnessing Fear

"Have I not commanded you?
Be strong and of good courage;
do not be afraid, nor be dismayed,
for the LORD your God is with you wherever you go."

JOSHUA 1:9 NKJV

Whatever we face, we never face it alone. The Lord our God is with us no matter where we are or where we go. We cannot outrun his presence; his love is our covering every day. When fear comes barging into our hearts, overcoming our nervous system, we are not left to deal with the anxiety on our own.

Be strong and take courage. You are not alone. Courage does not mean erasing fear from your mind; it is harnessing the energy behind it and choosing to keep doing the right thing. You need not rely on your own strength. The Spirit of the Lord is upon you; he pours out his grace that empowers you to choose him over and over again. Keep going!

Emmanuel, I know that you are the God who is present in my every moment. There's no need to fear any outcome when I know that you are with me. Lead me in your love and teach me with the clarity of your wisdom. As I press on, do more than I could think to ask you for. I cling to you.

Under the Surface

Grow in the grace and knowledge of our Lord and Savior Jesus Christ.
To him be glory both now and forever! Amen.
2 PETER 3:18 NIV

No matter how much we know about the Lord and his ways, there is always more to discover. Though there are times in life that are naturally slower, there is still growth that happens. In the dormancy of winter, we can forget that there is purpose in dying. Though outward growth may be scarce, there is still much happening under the surface.

Are you in a winter season? Do you feel as if everything has slowed down and what you were once enjoying in abundance has been stripped down to what looks like barrenness? Do not be discouraged. There is rhythm to the cycle of life, of nature, and the seasons. There is still growth; you may simply need to look at it differently. Dig deep; it's there.

Jesus, I'm thankful for the reminder of the cycle of seasons in nature as it points me to the seasons of life. Help me to see where you are working under the surface. Though I may have to dig deeper to find it, I won't stop looking for evidence of your goodness.

Choose to Trust

When I am afraid,
I will put my trust in you.
PSALM 56:3 NLT

When we are afraid, we can still choose to put our trust in God.
It's not a question of if we're afraid; rather, it's a matter of when.
We can trust God in the stable, good times, and in the uncertainty
of sorrow and loss. Will we remember his unchanging character,
knowing that he will continue to be faithful to his Word?

Let today be the day we bind our hearts to God in expectation
even if we do it with fear and trembling. His peace will calm our
unsteady hearts. He is trustworthy. He is able. He is powerful. He is
present. He is fighting for us. He is not done with us yet, no matter
what the odds look like. He is victorious.

Worthy God, even when I am afraid, I will choose to trust you.
Don't let me go, Lord, and don't let me down. Blow me away
with your goodness and faithful mercy. You are so much better
than a fair-weather friend. You are my rock and my salvation,
and I put my confidence in you.

Places of Need

"Behold, I will bring to it health and healing,
and I will heal them and reveal
to them abundance of prosperity and security."
JEREMIAH 33:6 ESV

God reveals his love to us in a myriad of ways. His unrelenting kindness is not just a nice thought; he follows through with tangible acts of mercy. He is full of compassion for you. What areas of your life, your mind, your heart, or your body need a touch from the Healer?

Out of the abundance of his heart of love, God meets us with the power of his Spirit. Invite him into the places of need once again. His power has no restrictions and his love does not exclude any part of your life. Let the healer tend to your broken heart. He restores all things; he will make you new.

Healer, meet me in the depth of my need. I admit that I sometimes grow tired of asking for help, but that won't stop me today. Restore me like only you can, my Creator and my God. I trust you to do it. Heal me, and I will be healed.

Turn Your Thoughts

Think about the things that are good and worthy of praise.
Think about the things that are true and honorable
and right and pure and beautiful and respected.

PHILIPPIANS 4:8 NCV

What have your thoughts been filled with these days? Have you been consumed with the overwhelming reports of bad news in the world? Have you been overcome by your own pain, unable to focus on that which is still here and still good? This is not meant to shame you. Rather, let it be a reminder that you can turn your thoughts.

When we focus on things which are true, honorable, beautiful, and pure, our minds will know a greater peace than if we spend most of our mental energy on problems and suffering. This is not to say that we erase the pain, nor should we ignore it. However, let us look to him who embodies all mercy, kindness, and goodness. We cannot go wrong if we seek his perspective.

Wise God, as I look to you, teach me how to train my thoughts in submission to your loving nature. When I am overwhelmed by the destruction around me, give me eyes to see that you are still present, you are still faithful, and you are still good.

Responsible for Me

Every man's way is right in his own eyes,
But the LORD weighs the hearts.

PROVERBS 21:2 NASB

When it comes down to it, all we can do in this life is live our own lives. We cannot change others, though we may try. We cannot control every outcome, though we wish we could. We are ultimately responsible for our own actions, responses, and motivations of our hearts.

When we submit our lives to God, living for and from his love, our hearts will mold to his mercy and our lives will reflect the fruit of his Spirit. Let us refrain from judging others, and instead focus on what we can do to love them well in kindness, in humility, and in the likeness of Jesus.

All-knowing One, you see what no one else can—straight through our actions to the motivations of our hearts. Help me to keep my eyes fixed on you especially when I am tempted to judge my neighbor. May I remain humble in your love and remember that faith, hope, and love are the only things that will remain in the end.

A Bright Blessing

"The LORD bless you and keep you;
the LORD make his face shine on you and be gracious to you;
the LORD turn his face toward you and give you peace."

NUMBERS 6:24–26 NIV

As you read this blessing, may your heart open to the possibilities that are available to you in fellowship with God today. Turn it into a personal prayer. May the Spirit of the Lord wrap around your heart with comfort and the nearness of his love as you pray.

He is ever so close today. His mercy shines brightly on your life, and he is always leaning in with kindness toward you. Peace is your plentiful portion, for he is the Prince of Peace. He will bless and keep you, beloved.

Lord, will you bless me and keep me today? Will you make your face shine upon me and be gracious to me? Turn your face toward me and give me peace. You are the one I look to for all that I long for and for every need. Surround me with the light of your countenance.

A Father's Help

Give us a Father's help when we face our enemies.
For to trust in any man is an empty hope.
PSALM 108:12 TPT

Even the most loyal friends will sometimes disappoint us. The dependability of others is limited, but God is endless in strength and power. He will always provide a Father's help when we need it. The fullness of his love is working on our behalf. He will not let us be crushed, he won't let us be ashamed, and he won't let us be destroyed.

Let our deepest trust not be in any strength that the world advertises. May it be in the faithfulness and mercy-power of the living God, who is also our good Father. He will not disappoint us. He is better than any other love we've ever known. So much better.

Father, I know that you have not abandoned me in my sorrow and pain. Lift my head today, that I may see where you are working for my good. Don't let me be swayed by the lies of better life outside of you. You will not fail me. Open my eyes again.

A Distant Memory

I consider that our present sufferings are not worth comparing with the glory that will be revealed in us.

ROMANS 8:18 NIV

Whatever you are going through today, remember that it is temporary. Though you suffer in seasons through this life, there is coming a day and an age where it will be but a distant memory. There is incomparable glory awaiting you in the everlasting kingdom of God.

This God, who gives beauty for ashes, joy for mourning, and the spirit of praise for heaviness, is with you now and will not leave you. When you consider the joys you have experienced in this life, they are just a foretaste of the unparalleled beauty that you will dwell in when you are face-to-face with your Creator and Savior. Hold on; there is so much more to come.

Holy One, keep my heart rooted in your constant love that leads me straight to your heart. Keep my eyes fixed on you, so no matter what troubles I face here, I may remember that it does not compare in the slightest to the glorious freedom and light of your everlasting kingdom.

Finished Work

By grace you have been saved through faith;
and that not of yourselves, it is the gift of God;
not as a result of works, so that no one may boast.
EPHESIANS 2:8–9 NASB

What wonderful news, that reconciliation with God is his work, and not what we could ever offer on our own. Jesus already paved the way to the Father, breaking down every barrier, and disarming every claim of shame. Salvation is not something we attain to; rather it is a finished work that we receive as a gift from the one who broke the power of sin and death.

We are not more worthy of mercy and kindness on our best days than we are on our worst. There is nothing that can qualify us for unhindered relationship with God because it has never been about what we do. We have been grafted into a loving family—the family of God. We belong because he says we do.

Gracious God, teach me to never put qualifications on my own worth or any other's. You have accepted me as I am, and I want to do the same with those in my life. You are wonderful—so, so wonderful. I quit my striving today and simply accept the fact that you love me as I am.

Not a Disappointment

As a father has compassion on his children,
so the Lord has compassion on those who fear him.
PSALM 103:13 NIV

When you feel as if you've run out of chances, remember that God is full of mercy and constant in compassion. You cannot ever exhaust his love. It doesn't matter the number of bad moods or bad days you have had. You are his beloved child, and he is not going to turn away from you.

What areas of your life are you drained by? Though you disappoint yourself, you are not a disappointment to your Father. He knows you better than you know yourself, and he is full of kindness, wisdom, and strength for you in every single circumstance. Take rest in his affection today and let him lead you in love.

Compassionate One, I'm so grateful that your standards are better than my own and much more gracious. Even when I fall and fail, it does not make me a failure. Speak your words of life over me again, and remind me who I am and even more who you are.

No Exceptions

Love is patient,
love is kind.
It does not envy,
it does not boast,
it is not proud.

1 CORINTHIANS 13:4 NIV

How easy it can be to put qualifications on love based on our expectations of others. But that is not how the love of God works. God's love makes no exceptions for who can receive it or how much they get. His mercy-love is humble, it is patient, and it is kind.

Love does not resent others, nor does it brag about what it does. Love is not full of itself. Though in our humanity, we take offense, God's love does not. Love keeps no record of wrongs, nor does it compare itself to others. God's love is pure in its intent. He loves because he is love. There are no exclusions.

Loving God, I can hardly comprehend the framework of your love let alone its immensity. Who is like you in lovingkindness? I can't think of one person who exhibits the purity of your love without misstep. I submit myself to the overwhelming mercy of your heart. Help me to align myself with your love and keep my heart humble.

Look at the Time

For everything there is a season,
and a time for every matter under heaven.
ECCLESIASTES 3:1 NRSV

God is working behind the scenes of your story. Though you may not understand his timing, it does not mean that he has abandoned you or his plans for your life. He is still the master redeemer and restorer. He is the one who first called you in lovingkindness, and who keeps you covered in that same sea of mercy today.

It is wisdom to look at the times and to discern what kind of season you are currently in. Though you may be walking through hardship, enduring the heartache of loss, the intensity of your pain will not always be so great. God is walking with you, making a way for you where there seems to be none. Trust him with your present; his kindness has not run out.

Perfect Father, give me eyes to see what season I am in. Give my heart understanding of what you are doing in me during this time. Above all, weave my heart into your own so I may be intricately intertwined with your love no matter the times or seasons.

A Wonderful Reality

A child has been born to us; God has given a son to us.
He will be responsible for leading the people.
His name will be Wonderful Counselor, Powerful God,
Father Who Lives Forever, Prince of Peace.

ISAIAH 9:6 NCV

Jesus is our leader now and forevermore. As we look to the first coming of God in human form, may we be reminded of his innate love and mercy. May we look upon the humble life that Jesus led and the powerful ministry of his later years. May we remember that God with us also means God leading us.

What a wonderful reality, that Jesus is the Son of God and Son of Man. He is both. We can know him in our humanity, as well as in the power of his love poured out on us in Spirit and in truth. He is the Prince of Peace. He is the powerful God; he is our Wonderful Counselor. Hallelujah!

Prince of Peace, I look to the wonder of your first coming, and it fills my heart with anticipation for your second. I long for the day when the veil is lifted from my eyes and I can fully take you in, not in part, but in whole. Lead me, Lord. You are worthy of my trust.

The Anticipated Messiah

"Today in the town of David a Savior has been born to you;
he is the Messiah, the Lord."

LUKE 2:11 NIV

Jesus is the fulfillment of the Old Testament law. He was the awaited Messiah—the kinsman-redeemer that all of Israel anticipated. He did not come with swords or awe-inspiring power. He was born in a stable, surrounded by animals as a refugee. He was not home, and yet he came to show us the way to our forever home.

May we remember the humanity of Jesus as much as we recall the overcoming power of Christ's ministry. He was acquainted with suffering; he was a humble carpenter. He was not born of earthly kings, but he was the King of kings, even in the humility of his flesh and bones. Messiah has come. He has led us to life in unhindered relationship with the Father. He is our help today. The Messiah is alive, and he is with us in Spirit.

Emmanuel, today I remember who you are. You did not stay seated on your glory-throne and spout orders to angels to help your people. You came in humble form as one of us. You lived as a man with all of man's limitations. And yet, you overcame death and the grave. You are my Messiah, and I worship you.

Rushing Cleansing Waters

*"He who believes in Me, as the Scripture has said,
out of his heart will flow rivers of living water."*
JOHN 7:38 NKJV

Even in the midst of suffering, when our hope is diminished and our strength is small, there is access to the rivers of God's living waters of grace. When our lives are submitted to Christ, his mercy-tide flows freely into our lives and out of our hearts.

Whatever your emotional state today, God is with you and his Word is alive in you. The life that he offers through his Spirit, you cannot diminish. He will provide for your every need, and you will know his tangible goodness in the way his mercy moves in your life. Fill up on his kindness, for there is more than you could ever consume available to you.

God of abundance, I trust that you will never stop your love from flowing toward me. I turn toward you again today; meet me with the rushing cleansing waters of your mercy. Refresh my weary soul. You are my God, and I belong to you.

Giving Up Judgment

"If you forgive those who sin against you,
your heavenly Father will forgive you.
But if you refuse to forgive others,
your Father will not forgive your sins."
MATTHEW 6:14–15 NLT

There is power in forgiveness. When we choose to extend mercy instead of judgment, our hearts are free to receive the same. When we withhold it, we are not harming anyone but ourselves. The punishment of refusing to offer compassion is our own; it does not affect the one whom we think it would.

Forgiveness is not ignoring the hurt that was caused, but it does let go of the need for controlled consequences. There are natural consequences to actions taken, but not all can be dictated. Our power lies in the depths of our ability to extend mercy to others. God, who is perfect in love and justice, will be our advocate and defense when we have no other. Will we let him take that role and give up our own harsh judgments?

Merciful God, teach me how to loosen my grip especially around hurts and offenses. As I practice showing mercy to others, let my understanding of your mercy grow. You are so kind and patient. Thank you for that. Teach me to trust your leadership.

Greatest Confidence

The LORD will be your confidence,
And will keep your foot from being caught.
PROVERBS 3:26 NASB

Where does your greatest confidence lie? Is it in your own strength and abilities? Is it in the reliability of your loved ones? Is it in the promises made by those in leadership? Surely, as long as we are human and walking this aging earth, we will be let down by people—even ourselves.

Let us look again at the faithfulness of God. Let us read the Word of his promises and search out how he showed up for his people time and time again. Let us remember how he has done the same for us. Let us take heart and take hope in his unchanging character. May God and God alone be our great confidence.

Constant One, you have never failed to follow through on your Word. May I find my greatest confidence in you. Do not stop moving in my life; lead me on in your steadfast goodness. You are the hope that keeps me going. Lead me on the path of life for as long as I live. I will praise you.

Making Things Right

After you suffer for a short time, God, who gives all grace, will make everything right. He will make you strong and support you and keep you from falling. He called you to share in his glory in Christ, a glory that will continue forever.

1 PETER 5:10 NCV

Suffering will not last forever. The acute pain of sorrow will not always overwhelm our senses. This is not to diminish its impact or the hard road that we walk upon. But it is not the end. God will make everything right. He will set the lonely in families, he will restore what was lost, and he will revive the dead.

There is unlimited strength to be found in him. He is our support who keeps us from falling. He is the shining light of our lives, and he will never leave us. He is everything: the fulfillment of every longing, and the source of life, goodness, and pure love. Knowing him is its own reward—the greatest reward.

Righteous One, I know that you are not finished working out your redemption in the earth. One day you will wipe every tear from each and every eye and declare the never-ending peace of your reign. How I long for that day. But until then, I press into knowing you more.

Remain Fixed

Teach us to number our days,
that we may gain a heart of wisdom.
PSALM 90:12 NIV

When we experience loss, we cannot escape the reality of the limits of this life. What a gift we are given in the expansion of our understanding. Do we not look differently to others when we see through the eyes of suffering? We cannot escape the compassion that deepens our consideration of others who also suffer.

There is wisdom in understanding that our days are limited. Though life is short, the impact of perfect love's redemption is not small. May we walk in the light of God's mercy and kindness for as long as our feet tread this dusty earth. May our eyes remain fixed on Jesus, the one who was, and is, and is to come.

Wise God, I look to you through the good times and the hard. May I always remember the limits of this small life, that I may choose wisely to love when I have the opportunity. Fill me with the mercy of your heart, that I may offer the same kindness to those walking the road of suffering.

Cultivating Life

"Behold, I am doing a new thing;
now it springs forth, do you not perceive it?
I will make a way in the wilderness
and rivers in the desert."

ISAIAH 43:19 ESV

In the dawning of a new year, there is plenty to both reflect on and look forward to. As we look back on the last year, may we have eyes to see where God was with us and where he was cultivating life where we could only see destruction. Where was his hand of mercy present?

As we look ahead, may our hearts stir with the hope of good things to come. God is always doing a new thing, for his works and wonders are living and active. He did not stop working in the world after Jesus resurrected from the dead. He is here with us now, and he is speaking a better word. May we follow him on the path of life as he continues to make a way for us.

Worthy One, I will continue to follow you as you lead me into the unknown. You are kind, loving, and true. Your presence sustains me. Lead me on in perfect love and continue to redeem my story for your glory and for my good.